A World of Fiction

1

FIRST EDITION

TIMELESS SHORT STORIES

Sybil Marcus
University of California, Berkeley

Daniel Berman

A World of Fiction 1

Copyright © 2014 by Pearson Education, Inc.
All rights reserved.

Pearson Education, 10 Bank Street, White Plains, NY 10606

Staff Credits: The people who made up the *A World of Fiction 1* team—representing editorial,
production, design, and manufacturing—are Tracey Munz Cataldo, Rosa Chapinal, Aerin Csigay,
Daniel Dwyer, Nancy Flaggman, Amy McCormick, Joan Poole, and Jane Townsend.

Development: Page Designs International
Project management and text composition: S4Carlisle Publishing Services
Cover photo: "Mountain Sentinel" by Ronald H. Berman
Text font: Palatino LT Std Roman

Library of Congress Cataloging-in-Publication Data
A World of Fiction 1 : Timeless Short Stories / [compiled by] Sybil Marcus, University of California, Berkeley;
Daniel Berman. —First Edition.
    pages cm
 ISBN 978-0-13-304616-8
 1. English language—Textbooks for foreign speakers.   2. Short stories.   I. Marcus, Sybil.
II. Berman, Daniel.
 PE1128.W7598 2014
 428.6′4—dc23
                                                                                         2013047629

For text credits, please turn to the back of the book.

Printed in the United States of America

ISBN 10: 0-13-304616-8
ISBN 13: 978-0-13-304616-8

2 17

Dedication

To Ellen,
A loving presence in our lives, whose passion for the arts inspires

Brief Contents

Contents

Moments of Discovery   55

Paths to Adulthood   169

Preface

It is with great pleasure that Daniel Berman and I introduce this new level in the *World of Fiction* series: *A World of Fiction 1*.

The original *A World of Fiction*, now published in its third edition under the new title *A World of Fiction 2*, is aimed at the most advanced ESL/EFL students. Over the years, the book has resonated with many teachers who share my passion for placing literature at the center of language study. A number of these teachers have requested a companion textbook that would be appropriate for high-intermediate classrooms. *A World of Fiction 1* has been written in response to such requests.

The stories at this level have been chosen with a careful eye toward length and difficulty, but the guiding principle remains the same as for *A World of Fiction 2*: to present a selection that is challenging but accessible, and to guide students systematically through each story's literary, linguistic, and cultural layers.

I have used short fiction now for four decades in the classroom. As an ESL/EFL tool, the story has proven itself magnificently. Its form offers nonnative students a complete work of literature with the essential elements of character, setting, plot, motive, and theme, but with a brevity that is nonthreatening. Short stories present the opportunity to reflect on a number of different subjects during a limited course of study, as well as to grapple with a variety of styles that all represent English used in an authentic way. In the process, students enhance their reading, speaking, writing, grammar, and vocabulary skills in a sophisticated and engaging way.

This book arises from the conviction that literature in ESL/EFL education is not just a means to an end, but rather that close scrutiny of a fine literary text is a richly satisfying and rewarding endeavor in itself. We encourage students to think of themselves as archaeologists whose aim is to dig out the buried meanings in the text. In the process, students of English will sharpen their critical thinking and heighten their intercultural sensitivity as they come to understand that there are universal truths and sentiments that bind us all. The stories in this collection offer so many avenues of attack, so many opportunities for curiosity and excitement, that they will naturally inspire even the shyest students to think, discuss, compare, and debate.

Each chapter in *A World of Fiction 1* is based on an unabridged short story. The stories are loosely grouped into four thematic sections: *Denying the Truth*, *Moments of Discovery*, *Choices*, and *Paths to Adulthood*. Since these categories are elastic, a story can easily fit into more than one grouping. Within each section, the stories are ordered from easier to more challenging.

Chapters are divided into five parts that cover the full array of reading, critical thinking, and oral skills, as well as grammar, vocabulary, and writing. The book is designed to be used flexibly, so teachers should feel free to select chapters according to their own requirements and interests.

An underlying premise of our approach is that students read each story twice at home, making full use of the word glosses as they familiarize themselves with the plot and themes. At this level, we encourage students to respond freshly and individually to each story. Therefore, there are no prereading questions that alert the students to the story's content, although the capsule summary under the title does provide a clue. Teachers who prefer a more directed method may point students in advance to the *Thinking About the Story* section, which contains a question designed to promote thought and discussion.

After a first reading, students should be equipped with the vocabulary to understand and discuss the plot, while after a second reading they are poised to explore the story's themes. They can then move on to consider the distinctive style of the piece. After this, students are led to express their judgments on the characters' decisions, as well as to ponder the larger issues through their individual cultural prisms.

The transition to studying a story's grammar and vocabulary is a smooth one, as students generally find it much easier to absorb and implement grammatical and lexical items that they have encountered in context. Finally, students should be ready to write short essays in which they integrate what they have learned.

Raymond Carver, one of the authors in this book, addressed the magic of great short fiction when he said: "It's possible, in a poem or short story, to write about commonplace things and objects using commonplace but precise language, and to endow those things—a chair, a window curtain, a fork, a stone, a woman's earring—with immense, even startling power."

We hope that teachers who adopt literature in their classrooms will discover with us that it is a particularly effective way of imparting language skills. We hope too that as students engage with the stories in this volume, they find their efforts rewarded not only by improved English-language abilities, but also by unexpected insights into art, culture, and life.

How to Use This Book

Each chapter in this anthology is based on a complete short story and is divided into five sections, which call upon the diverse language and critical thinking skills of the student.

Part 1: First Reading

A. Thinking About the Story

Students are encouraged to express their visceral responses to the story. The aim is to stimulate an immediate and personal reaction in which students relate to a character or situation.

B. Understanding the Plot

The questions in this section lead students through the story in chronological order, eliciting their understanding of its characters, events, motive, and setting. Students who experience difficulties with a story during their first reading may wish to refer to these questions to guide them as they read. This section may be completed orally or in writing, depending on the needs of the class.

Part 2: Critical Thinking

The critical thinking questions in this part of the chapter can be answered orally or in writing. We recommend that students first write their answers to the theme and style questions, and then share these answers with a partner or in a small group. The judgment and cross-cultural questions call for an oral response, as does the debate section. Students generally tend to benefit from sharing their thoughts and perspectives in a spirited exchange, whether in small groups or in a broader class discussion.

A. Exploring Themes

After reading the story a second time, students should be ready to tackle more demanding and substantive questions, which will expose the story's underlying meanings and universal truths.

B. Analyzing Style

This section highlights salient literary devices and elements of style, such as metaphor, smile, personification, point of view, inference, and irony. Students are required to analyze the ways in which an author uses language to reinforce themes and create a distinctive voice.

C. Judging for Yourself

The questions in this section allow students to adopt a more flexible approach to the text and to move beyond the limits of the story. Students may be encouraged to speculate about events that have not been spelled out or to judge the wisdom of a character's actions. Sometimes they are asked to reflect on possible solutions to problems raised in the story. This offers classes the opportunity to engage in conflict-resolution activities as students assess how the problems they have analyzed in the story might best be resolved.

D. Making Connections

If a class has a cross-cultural, multi-ethnic component, the questions in this section will encourage students to compare and contrast their views on controversial actions or standpoints in the story, using their own cultural and societal values as a touchstone. In a more homogeneous class, there are still rich opportunities to compare the group's common values with those expressed in the story, as well as to explore dissenting views within the class.

E. Debate

Part 2 ends with a debate. Partners debate the pros and cons of a topic question. By this stage, students should have acquired the necessary vocabulary and command of English to enable them to present their arguments forcefully.

Part 3: Grammar in Context

Part 3 offers students a chance to review and practice a particular aspect of grammar that arises organically in the story. Structures covered include adverbial and adjectival clauses, participles and participial phrases, gerunds and infinitives, contractions, wishes and hopes, modals, present and past tenses, articles, count and noncount nouns, and parallel structure.

Part 4: Vocabulary Building

In Part 4 students are asked to focus on a particular aspect of vocabulary that has arisen in the chapter. The exercises in this section are varied. They have been designed to be as engaging as possible and discourage rote learning. The words, phrases, and idioms selected for instruction have been chosen with an eye to helping students express themselves with greater nuance and sophistication.

Part 5: Writing Activities

By the time students arrive at this section, they will have carefully considered the story and its related topics, acquired a richer vocabulary, and refreshed their understanding of one or more grammatical structures. They are now equipped to tackle the writing assignments, which range from creative exercises to short analyses, interviews, personal essays, and movie or book reviews. In each chapter, one of the assignments asks students to practice the grammar or vocabulary they've been studying.

Acknowledgments

We are deeply grateful to the following people, whose help has been invaluable in the writing of this book.

Bernard Seal, our project manager, who guided us through this new addition to the series with knowledge, judgment, forbearance, and humor. He was a trusted pillar of strength from start to finish.

Joe Chapple, our development editor, whose experience, encouragement, and meticulous approach to detail kept us honest until we found the right words.

The following people at Pearson, who contributed to the production of this book with professionalism and care: Pietro Alongi, Tracey Munz Cataldo, Rosa Chapinal, Daniel Dwyer, Amy McCormick, Liza Pleva, Joan Poole, Massimo Rubini, and Jane Townsend.

Candace Khanna, Ellen Rosenfield, Jim Seger, and Brandon Spears at the University of California at Berkeley Summer English Language Studies, who gave us invaluable feedback on individual chapters.

Special thanks to Tom McNichol from the University of California at Berkeley Summer English Language Studies, who graciously tried out many stories and provided a wealth of commentary.

Ellen Rosenfield and Patti Weissman, who unstintingly answered many grammar questions with expertise.

Margi Ward, who generously gave Sybil carte blanche to test her new material at the University of California at Berkeley Summer English Language Studies.

Ron Berman, who supported us in countless loving ways.

Students from the 2012 and 2013 summer sessions at Berkeley, whose goodwill and hard work helped us decide which stories and exercises to use.

The many international students whose curiosity, openness, and enthusiasm have been an inspiration for thirty years.

DENYING THE TRUTH

Sleeping
Noel
Arrangement in Black and White
A Serious Talk

1 〜 Sleeping

Katharine Weber

(b. 1955)

Katharine Weber was born in New York City. She has worked as an editorial assistant, journalist, book reviewer, and teacher. Her first story, "Friend of the Family," appeared in the *New Yorker* in 1993. Her novels include *Objects in Mirror Are Closer Than They Appear* (1995), *Triangle* (2006), and *True Confections* (2010). Weber has also written a memoir, *The Memory of All That* (2011), about her unusual relatives. It describes her difficult movie-producer father and her factory-worker grandmother. It also includes an account of the affair between her songwriter grandmother and the composer George Gershwin. Weber currently works in the graduate writing program at Columbia University. In 1996 she was named one of the fifty best young American novelists by *Granta Magazine*.

Sleeping

A babysitter has a strange experience in her employer's house.

She would not have to change a diaper,[1] they said. In fact, she would not have to do anything at all. Mrs. Winter said that Charles would not wake while she and Mr. Winter were out at the movies. He was a very sound sleeper,[2] she said. No need to have a bottle for him or anything. Before the Winters left they said absolutely please not to look in on[3] the sleeping baby because the door squeaked too loudly.

Harriet had never held a baby, except for one brief moment, when she was about six, when Mrs. Antler next door had surprisingly bestowed on her[4] the tight little bundle that was their new baby, Andrea. Harriet had sat very still and her arms had begun to ache from the tension by the time Mrs. Antler took back her baby. Andy was now a plump seven-year-old, older than Harriet had been when she held her that day.

After two hours of reading all of the boring mail piled neatly on a desk in the bedroom and looking through a depressing wedding album filled with photographs of dressed-up people in desperate need of orthodonture[5] (Harriet had just ended two years in braces[6] and was very conscious of malocclusion issues[7]) while flipping channels[8] on their television, Harriet turned the knob on the baby's door very tentatively[9], but it seemed locked. She didn't dare turn the knob with more pressure because what if she made a noise and woke him and he started to cry?

She stood outside the door and tried to hear the sound of a baby breathing but she couldn't hear anything through the door except the sound of the occasional car that passed by on the street outside. She wondered what Charles looked like. She wasn't even sure how old he was. Why had she agreed to baby-sit when Mr. Winter approached her at the swim club? She had never seen him before, and it was flattering[10] that he took her for being capable, as if just being a girl her age automatically qualified her as a baby-sitter.

---

1 **change a diaper** put a new cloth on a baby's bottom
2 **He was a very sound sleeper.** He slept very deeply.
3 **look in on** briefly check on someone
4 **bestowed on her** handed her
5 **orthodonture** dentistry to correct irregular teeth
6 **braces** special wires used to straighten teeth
7 **malocclusion issues** problems with how the upper and lower teeth fit together
8 **flipping channels** changing television stations without thinking
9 **tentatively** cautiously
10 **flattering** complimentary

By the time the Winters came home, Harriet had eaten most of the M & M's[11] in the glass bowl on their coffee table: first all the blue ones, then the red ones, then all the green ones, and so on, leaving,
35 in the end, only the yellow.

They gave her too much money and didn't ask her about anything. Mrs. Winter seemed to be waiting for her to leave before checking on the baby. Mr. Winter drove her home in silence. When they reached her house he said, My wife. He hesitated, then he said,
40 You understand, don't you? and Harriet answered Yes without looking at him or being sure what they were talking about although she did really know what he was telling her and then she got out of his car and watched him drive away.

---

11 **M & M's** colorful chocolate candies

FIRST READING

A Thinking About the Story

Discuss the following question with a partner.

Do you think the Winters behaved fairly toward Harriet? Give reasons for your answer.

B Understanding the Plot

Be prepared to answer the following questions with a partner or your class.

1. About how old do you think Harriet is? Explain your answer.
2. What instructions does Harriet receive from the couple? Are these the usual instructions that a babysitter receives?
3. How does Harriet occupy her time at the Winters' house?
4. What does Harriet notice about the people in the wedding photographs? Why do they catch her attention?
5. What other photograph album would you expect Harriet to see in the Winters' house?
6. Why is it surprising that the Winters chose Harriet to babysit Charles?
7. Why did Harriet agree to babysit for the Winters?

8. Why do you think the Winters pay Harriet so generously?

9. What is strange about the Winters' behavior when they return home?

10. What does Mr. Winter mean when he says, "My wife . . . You understand, don't you?" (lines 39–40)

PART 2

CRITICAL THINKING

A Exploring Themes

Reread "Sleeping." Then answer the following questions, which explore the story more deeply.

1. Harriet comes to understand that the Winters do not really need someone to look after their baby. Explain why Mrs. Winter still insists on hiring a babysitter.

2. How would you describe Mr. Winter's personality? What is his role in the story?

3. How does the couple's name represent a theme in the story?

4. What kinds of privacy issues are raised in the story?

B Analyzing Style

POINT OF VIEW

When we read a story, we see the events through the eyes of the narrator. This perspective is called **point of view**. Sometimes the narrator is a character in the story; other times the narrator is unknown. It is important to remember that the narrator doesn't always tell the whole truth. We need to pay attention to anything the narrator might not know or understand, as well as to any prejudices he or she might have.

Most stories are narrated in the first person or the third person. Stories in the first person are told using the pronoun *I*. Stories in the third person are told using the pronouns *he*, *she*, and *they*. Stories are rarely narrated in the second person, using the pronoun *you* to address the reader directly.

"Sleeping" is told in the third person from the point of view of the young Harriet. We have access to her thoughts, but we can't see into the minds of the other characters. As a result, we have to rely on Harriet for our information. This influences our perspective on the events.

Answer the following questions.

1. Harriet's youth and inexperience cause her to miss several important signs that something is unusual about the situation. Give at least three examples.

2. If the story had been told from Mr. Winter's point of view, how might he have described the events? Similarly, if Mrs. Winter had told the story, what do you think she would have said?

C Judging for Yourself

Express yourself as personally as you like in your answers to the following questions.

1. Do you think the Winters will ask Harriet to babysit again? Why or why not?

2. In your opinion, did Harriet behave responsibly in the Winters' house?

3. What reasons can you think of for why the Winters have no baby? Which explanation do you think is most likely?

4. Mr. Winter doesn't challenge his wife's fantasy. Do you think he should?

D Making Connections

Answer the following questions in a small group.

1. How common is babysitting in your country? Who usually babysits?

2. In your society, how is a babysitter expected to behave? How are parents supposed to treat the babysitter?

3. In your country, at what age are children usually left alone by their parents?

E Debate

Decide whether you are for or against the following statement. Write several arguments that support your view. Share your points with a classmate who has taken the opposite position.

It is always better to face the truth.

ADVERBIAL CLAUSES

An **adverbial clause** is a type of dependent clause, meaning that it cannot be a sentence on its own. Adverbial clauses answer questions such as when, where, and why something happened. Like all clauses, they have a subject and a verb. Four of the more common types of adverbial clauses are clauses of **time**, of **place**, of **reason**, and of **concession**. These clauses begin with a subordinating conjunction such as *when, before, whenever, where, wherever, because, since, although,* or *even though.*

- An adverbial clause of **time** expresses when something happens.

  *Andy was now a plump seven-year-old, older than Harriet had been **when she held her that day**.* (lines 13–14)

  ***Before the Winters returned home**, Harriet looked in their bedroom.*

- An adverbial clause of **place** expresses where something happens.

  ***Wherever Mrs. Winter goes**, she is followed by the memory of Charles.*

  *People often display photographs **where guests can see them**.*

- An adverbial clause of **reason** expresses why something happens.

  *She didn't dare turn the knob with more pressure **because it might wake the baby**.* (adapted from lines 21–23)

  ***Since she was only a young girl**, Harriet was slow to understand the situation.*

- An adverbial clause of **concession** expresses contrast or a surprising result.

  *Harriet felt uneasy about Charles **although she couldn't explain why**.*

  ***Even though Mr. Winter paid her generously**, Harriet felt uncomfortable.*

Exercise 1

Underline the adverbial clause in each of the following sentences. Write the type of adverbial clause on the line following each sentence. The first one is done for you.

1. Charles did not wake up <u>while Mr. and Mrs. Winter were at the movies</u>.
   time

2. Mr. Winter warned Harriet not to open the door to Charles's bedroom because it squeaked too loudly. _____

3. When she was six years old, Harriet held a baby for the first time.
   _____

4. Harriet still felt hungry after she had eaten most of the M & Ms on the coffee table. _____

5. Although Harriet was at first puzzled by the Winters' behavior, she eventually understood it. _____

6. Since the door to the baby's room squeaked, Harriet was afraid to open it. _____

7. Wherever the Winters go, they look for a new babysitter.
_____

8. Harriet read the Winters' mail even though she felt guilty.
_____

9. Mr. Winter tried to explain the situation to Harriet before she got out of his car. _____

10. Harriet put the letters back where she had found them.
_____

PUNCTUATION OF ADVERBIAL CLAUSES

Clear rules govern the punctuation of adverbial clauses. Although authors do not always strictly follow these rules, you should use them in your writing.

When an adverbial clause comes before the independent clause, place a comma between the two clauses.

> ***While we are away***, *please don't open the bedroom door.*

When an adverbial clause is placed after the independent clause, do not use a comma.

> *Please don't open the bedroom door **while we are away**.*

Exercise 2

Look at the following sentences with adverbial clauses. Underline the adverbial clause. Where necessary, insert a comma.

1. Wherever there are young people you can find a babysitter.
2. Mr. Winter wanted to be honest with Harriet when they were in the car together.
3. Unless Harriet knows the parents she won't agree to babysit again.
4. She had looked at all the wedding photos before the Winters came home.
5. Since Harriet was a very young girl she lacked life experience.
6. Although Harriet knew it was wrong she couldn't stop herself from looking through the Winters' personal items.
7. Harriet tried to look into the baby's room because she was curious to see him.
8. While Harriet was in the Winters' house she almost disobeyed their instructions.

POLYSEMOUS WORDS

Two words are **polysemous** if they're spelled and pronounced the same way but have different meanings. They may also be different parts of speech.

> *He was a very* **sound** *sleeper, she said.* (line 4)

In this sentence, *sound* is an adjective meaning *deep*.

> *. . . she couldn't hear anything through the door except the* **sound** *of the occasional car that passed by on the street outside.* (lines 25–26)

In this sentence, *sound* is a noun meaning *noise*.

> *Listen carefully. I am going to give you some* **sound** *advice.*

In this sentence, *sound* is an adjective meaning *sensible*.

Exercise

Look at the following pairs of sentences. With the help of a dictionary, explain the difference between the italicized words in each pair.

1. **a.** She would not have to *change* a diaper, they said. (line 1)

   b. The shop assistant gave me the wrong *change*.

2. **a.** . . . the door *squeaked* too loudly. (lines 6–7)

   b. She just *squeaked through* each month on her low salary.

3. **a.** Mrs. Antler . . . bestowed on her the *tight* little bundle that was their new baby. (lines 9–11)

   b. Money is *tight* these days.

4. **a.** Harriet spent two hours reading all of the *boring* mail piled neatly on a desk in the bedroom. (adapted from lines 15–16)

   b. The bank robbers took a long time *boring* through the lock.

5. **a.** Harriet looked through a *depressing* wedding album filled with photographs of people in desperate need of orthodonture. (adapted from lines 16–18)

   b. The government has failed to fix the problems *depressing* the economy.

6. **a.** Harriet spent quite a bit of time *flipping* through channels on their television. (adapted from lines 19–20)

   b. We decided that *flipping* a coin was the best way to choose who would go first.

7. **a.** She didn't dare turn the knob with more *pressure* . . . (lines 21–22)

   b. I do my best work under *pressure*.

PART 5

WRITING ACTIVITIES

1. Imagine you are Harriet and you open the door to the baby's bedroom. Say what you find. Describe your feelings before and after entering the room. Try to use a few adverbial clauses in your narrative.

2. In your country, is it common for teenagers to earn money by doing jobs like babysitting, gardening, or working part-time in stores? If so, write two paragraphs explaining what jobs are available and which are the most desirable. Indicate whether there's a difference between the jobs usually done by boys and by girls. If teenagers don't usually look for jobs, explain why not.

3. The novel *The Babysitter* by R. L. Stine is about a teenager who is threatened by an unknown telephone caller every time she babysits at a particular house. As in "Sleeping," the girl doesn't know the couple well, and the atmosphere of horror and suspense builds with each new phone call. Write a brief report on a book you have read or a movie or television episode you have seen that features a babysitter. Describe the plot and say what you thought about the book or movie.

2 🖋 Noel

Michael Plemmons

(b. 1951)

Michael Plemmons was born to a military family in Nevada. As a result he moved frequently as a child, attending thirteen schools across the United States and Europe. He earned a bachelor's degree in history from the University of South Alabama and a master's in journalism from Northwestern University. As a journalist, Plemmons wrote on a variety of subjects ranging from professional football to crime, government, and the arts. His literary works include short stories and the historical novel *Fianna* (2010). *Fianna* tells the story of a little-known plan to invade Canada during the U.S. Civil War. Plemmons compares writing to carpentry, saying, "It's a skilled trade. Every new story is a job site."

Noel[1]

A group of children experience Christmas in an unusual way.

Mrs. Hathaway brought the children downstairs single file[2] and seated them on straight-back chairs around the reception room, boy-girl-boy-girl, seventeen in all. In the corner stood a robust[3] Christmas tree bedecked with candy
5 canes and tinsel tresses.[4] The air was thick with the scent of pine and furniture polish as a phantom choir sang "Noel" to the strains of a vinyl disc orchestra.[5] Mrs. Hathaway was still fussing over their appearance, fixing the boys' neckties and correcting the girls' posture, when the first couple arrived. In hushed tones they spoke
10 with Mrs. Overton at the front desk. "We were thinking about a girl," said the woman. Mrs. Overton smiled broadly and made a sweeping motion with her hand. "We have a wonderful selection of girls," she said. At this the girls came to attention[6] in their places, each freckle[7] blooming on rosy cheeks. And as Mrs. Hathaway
15 presented them, each one stood and curtsied on cue.[8] "Christa is a lovely child, age eight . . . Melinda has a beautiful singing voice for carols . . . Stephanie has an exceptionally sweet temperament. . . ."

The clients turned to Mrs. Overton and quietly indicated their choice. She nodded, poker-faced,[9] and prepared the papers.
20 Money changed hands. The girls eyed each other nervously as Mrs. Overton recited the rental stipulations:[10] "You understand that this is only a 48-hour agreement. The girl must be returned by noon on the day after Christmas or late charges will be assessed at ten dollars per hour and you will forfeit[11] the insurance deposit." When
25 everything was in order she looked over at Mrs. Hathaway and said, "Melinda, please." A little squeak of joy escaped into the room as Melinda jumped up and rushed to join her hosts for the holiday. The other girls watched her go, their hope renewing as another pair of patrons entered the room from the foyer.[12]

---

1 **Noel** Christmas
2 **single file** one after another
3 **robust** healthy
4 **bedecked with candy canes and tinsel tresses** decorated with Christmas candy and shiny strips of metal
5 **a phantom choir sang "Noel" to the strains of a vinyl disc orchestra** a record of a Christmas song was playing

6 **came to attention** sat up straight, ready for instructions
7 **freckle** small brown dot on the skin
8 **curtsied on cue** bent their knees in a polite greeting when directed
9 **poker-faced** showing no expression
10 **stipulations** rules
11 **forfeit** give up
12 **foyer** entrance hallway

30 Throughout the afternoon they came two by two, childless on Christmas Eve. They were high-rise dwellers and they were pensioners from South Side bungalows. A few were first-timers, uneasy, unable to meet the children's eyes.[13] (The repeat customers, who each year made up a majority of the business, had reserved
35 their "Kristmas Kid" by name, weeks in advance, and had come by in the morning for express pick-up.) Most of those now arriving to browse among the leftovers[14] were last minute shoppers.

The girls were in great demand,[15] especially the youngest candidates in curls. Dimples and bangs,[16] once again, were very
40 popular. And for the boys, missing teeth and cowlicks[17] were favorite features. Considering the irregular inventory,[18] business was good. Of the original lot, only two rather plain-looking lads remained at six o'clock, closing time. Both bore the stigma of a pubescent mustache.[19]
45 Mrs. Overton finished her filing while Mrs. Hathaway affixed the "Closed" sign on the door, unplugged the Christmas lights, and drew the window shades all around. The boys sat silent, watchful.

Said Mrs. Overton, "I told you about those two pre-teens, didn't I?"
50 "Yes, ma'am, you did."

"Then why did you bring them down with the others?"

"Well, I was hoping, I guess." Mrs. Hathaway glanced at her rejected charges.[20] They gazed guiltily into their laps. "It did no harm to give them at least a chance."
55 Mrs. Overton regarded her for a moment, then answered calmly, "I suppose not." She was pleased with the day's proceeds,[21] too pleased to argue over a minor transgression.[22] Anyway, she did not want to discourage a certain degree of compassion, believing it was one of the qualities that made
60 Mrs. Hathaway an effective matron.[23]

---

13 **unable to meet the children's eyes** embarrassed to look directly at the children (idiom)

14 **browse among the leftovers** go through the last remaining items at a sale

15 **in great demand** very popular

16 **dimples and bangs** cute smiles and hair falling over the forehead

17 **cowlicks** hair standing up straight (as if licked by a cow)

18 **irregular inventory** imperfect items in a store

19 **bore the stigma of a pubescent mustache** showed some undesirable facial hair

20 **her rejected charges** the boys who were left behind

21 **the day's proceeds** the profits for that day

22 **a minor transgression** the breaking of an unimportant rule

23 **matron** woman in charge of children in an institution

Outside it was beginning to snow. Before leaving, Mrs. Overton wrapped herself in a muffler and donned a woolen cap. "I'll see you day after tomorrow then."

"Goodnight, ma'am," said Mrs. Hathaway, then turning to the
65 boys. "Come along."

As they slowly ascended the stairs, one of the boys emitted a peculiar nasal sound, a congested sentiment[24] perhaps.

"Quiet, child," said Mrs. Hathaway.

---

24 **a congested sentiment** an emotion difficult
to hide

FIRST READING

A Thinking About the Story

Discuss the following question with a partner.

> Were you surprised by the way Christmas is explored in this story? Explain your answer.

B Understanding the Plot

Be prepared to answer the following questions with a partner or your class.

1. Where does the story take place? Who are the children?
2. Who are Mrs. Hathaway and Mrs. Overton? How are their personalities different?
3. What does the reception room in the opening paragraph look like? Give as many details as possible.
4. Who are the *clients*? (line 18) What do they want?
5. What do you think the children are being compared to in lines 22–24? What expressions emphasize the comparison?
6. How long are the children allowed to be away?
7. To whom does the pronoun *they* refer in line 30?
8. Give two differences between the new and the returning clients.
9. Who are the two children left over at the end? Why were they rejected?
10. Why does Mrs. Hathaway unplug the Christmas lights? (line 46)
11. What was Mrs. Hathaway hoping for? (line 52)
12. Why is Mrs. Overton displeased that Mrs. Hathaway brought down the two boys? Why does she change her mind?

A Exploring Themes

Reread "Noel." Then answer the following questions, which explore the story more deeply.

1. Look at lines 1–7 and lines 45–47. For whom is the room really decorated? How is this important to the story's message about Christmas?

2. How is the commercialization of Christmas (using Christmas to make money) expressed in lines 30–37? Explain your answer.

3. Why do you think some of the couples are "unable to meet the children's eyes"? (line 33)

4. How do the children seem to feel about spending Christmas with strangers? Discuss the possible pros and cons.

B Analyzing Style

IRONY

Irony refers to a contrast between the surface of a story and the reality underneath. In order to understand irony, we need to look beyond the literal meaning of the text.

One common form of irony occurs when a character says something that seems to mean one thing but that actually means something very different. For example, when Mrs. Overton says, "We have a wonderful selection of girls" (lines 12–13), she sounds happy about it; in contrast, we as readers are struck by the cruelty of comparing children to items in a store.

Another form of irony occurs when a reader or a character expects one thing to happen, but the opposite occurs. For example, at the beginning of "Noel," the writer paints a picture of a warm holiday scene by including details associated with Christmas. However, we soon learn that the Christmas spirit is completely absent in the story. There is a moment of surprise when we suddenly see the contrast between what we expected and what's really there.

Exercise

Answer the following questions.

1. How is the title of the story ironic?

2. What is ironic about the couples' desire to take home a child for Christmas?

3. Explain the meaning of this sentence: *Considering the irregular inventory, business was good.* (lines 41–42) What is ironic about it?

4. Find two more examples of irony in the story.

C Judging for Yourself

Express yourself as personally as you like in your answers to the following questions.

1. What do you think of the couples who decide to rent a child for Christmas?

2. Do you think Mrs. Hathaway made a mistake in bringing the two older boys downstairs?

3. If the children enjoy themselves, do you think it is wrong to rent them out for Christmas? Explain your answer.

D Making Connections

Answer the following questions in a small group.

1. In the United States, Christmas and many other holidays have become commercialized. This means that the emphasis is on buying and selling items like flowers, greeting cards, and presents. How commercialized are holidays in your culture? Pick one holiday and describe it.

2. What is the situation of children who lose their parents in your country? Are they adopted, cared for by other members of their family, or placed in an institution?

3. In your country, what physical features are considered cute or attractive in children? Is it different for boys and girls?

E Debate

Decide whether you are for or against the following statement. Write several arguments that support your view. Share your points with a classmate who has taken the opposite position.

Companies should not take advantage of religious holidays to make money.

PRESENT AND PAST PARTICIPLES

The **participle** is related to a verb but functions as an adjective. Like an adjective, it modifies a noun or pronoun. The **present participle** always ends in *–ing*; the **past participle** often ends in *–ed*, but for irregular verbs it can have other endings such as *–t, –d, –en, –n,* or *–ne*. In the following sentences, the participle is in **bold** and the word it modifies is underlined.

> *Mrs. Overton smiled broadly and made a* **sweeping** motion *with her hand.*
> (lines 11–12)
> *Mrs. Hathaway glanced at her* **rejected** charges. *(lines 52–53)*

The present participle shows that the noun it modifies is doing the action. In contrast, the past participle shows that the noun it modifies is having the action done to it. It is important to use the right participle. To see why, look at how the participle affects the meaning in each of the following sentences:

> *I was* **boring** *during the lecture.* [I was a bad speaker.]
>
> *I was* **bored** *during the lecture.* [I was listening to a bad speaker.]
>
> *The lecture was* **boring**. [The content of the lecture was dull.]
>
> *The lecture was* **bored**. [Incorrect: A lecture can't have feelings.]
>
> *It was an* **embarrassing** *situation for him.* [The situation made him feel ashamed.]
>
> *The* **embarrassed** *man hid his face.* [The man felt ashamed.]
>
> *It was an* **embarrassed** *situation for him.* [Incorrect: A situation cannot have feelings, only a person can.]

Exercise 1

Look at the following sentences. Complete each sentence with the correct participle in parentheses.

1. I loved going to the play last night. It was a _____ experience. (satisfying/satisfied)

2. We get very _____ when our baby sister cries during the night. (annoying/annoyed)

3. It was a very _____ day for me yesterday. I worked for eleven hours. (tiring/tired)

4. I was so _____ in the lecture that I nearly fell asleep. (boring/bored)

5. He was an _____ person to meet. (interesting/
interested)

6. After eating a delicious meal, I felt very _____.
(satisfying/satisfied)

7. Getting lost in the wilderness was a _____
experience. (terrifying/terrified)

8. My father was a _____ person after his divorce.
(changing/changed)

9. My dog gave an _____ bark when he saw me return.
(exciting/excited)

10. I was a witness to the _____ airplane crash.
(horrified/horrifying)

11. It was such a _____ day when I missed my
graduation. I was very _____. (disappointing/
disappointed)

12. She looked _____ by this morning's news.
(troubling/troubled)

PARTICIPIAL PHRASES

A **participial phrase** consists of a present or past participle plus any related words, such as objects or adverbs. Like a participle, the participial phrase functions as an adjective. Participial phrases can be placed at the beginning, in the middle, or at the end of a sentence. To avoid confusion in your writing, it helps to put the participial phrase as close as possible to the noun or pronoun it modifies.

*At this the girls came to attention in their places, each <u>freckle</u> **blooming on rosy cheeks.*** (lines 13–14)

*In the corner stood a robust <u>Christmas tree</u> **bedecked with candy canes and tinsel tresses.*** (lines 3–5)

Exercise 2

Look at the following sentences. Underline the participial phrase. Circle the noun it modifies.

1. The children laughed at the sight of the Christmas tree lit with sparkling tinsel tresses.

2. The couples choosing their young guests look very happy.

3. The presents wrapped in colored paper were reserved for the girls.

4. The little girl sitting alone looked for someone to play with.

5. Showing their missing teeth, the boys smiled hopefully at the couples.

6. Mrs. Overton looked coldly at the older boys walking shyly into the room.

7. The couples disappointed with the leftovers didn't stay long.

8. The last Christmas lights shining weakly on the tree went out one by one.

9. The two boys left behind looked very unhappy.

10. Mrs. Overton watched the boys going up the stairs.

PART 4 # VOCABULARY BUILDING

BUSINESS EXPRESSIONS

"Noel" contains expressions related to business and shopping. For example, some of the couples know that they can save time by using *express pick-up* (line 36) to avoid waiting in line.

Exercise 1

Look at the following list of business expressions from the story. Using the glossary or a dictionary, make sure you understand each expression. Complete the sentences that follow with the appropriate expression.

selection (line 12)	repeat customers (line 33)
money changed hands (line 20)	browse among the leftovers (line 37)
rental stipulations (line 21)	inventory (line 41)
forfeit the deposit (line 24)	the day's proceeds (lines 56–57)

1. The toy store owner was disappointed with _____, especially since it was the holiday season.

2. Big stores try to attract _____ by sending out emails advertising their annual sale.

3. It is expensive to keep around lots of extra _____, so most stores try not to have more than they can sell.

4. Last-minute Christmas shoppers must _____ for their gifts.

5. _____ make it quite difficult for people under twenty-five to lease cars.

6. Sometimes a small but well-chosen _____
   can be good, since many shoppers have trouble making a decision when there
   are too many options.

7. If you damage this car in any way, you will have to

   _____.

8. After each sale, _____.

MONEY PROVERBS

A proverb is a short saying that contains a lesson about life. Many proverbs in
English have messages related to money.

Exercise 2

The following proverbs all refer to money. With a partner, first guess the
meaning of the proverbs. Then, check your answers in a dictionary of sayings
or on the Internet.

1. A fool and his money are soon parted.
2. Beggars can't be choosers.
3. Money doesn't grow on trees.
4. Money is power.
5. Time is money.
6. You can't take it with you.

Exercise 3

Share with your classmates another proverb you know that deals with
money. You may choose a proverb from any language.

PART 5 ## WRITING ACTIVITIES

1. Imagine it is the day after the children have returned. Pick two
   characters from the story and write a conversation between them
   about what happened over Christmas. Possible choices might include
   Mrs. Overton and Mrs. Hathaway, two of the children, or one of the
   couples. Try to use some participles and participial phrases in the
   conversation.

2. A well-known proverb says, *Money is the root of all evil*. First explain the
   proverb. Then write a paragraph in which you take a position for or
   against that statement. Compare your paragraph with a partner.

3. Many films portray the Christmas season. Classic movies and TV specials with optimistic messages, such as *It's a Wonderful Life* (1946) and *A Charlie Brown Christmas* (1965), represent the traditional Christmas spirit. As a result, these films and TV programs are repeatedly shown during the holiday season. Other films, like the documentary *What Would Jesus Buy?* (2007), take a more critical look at the holiday. Choose a movie about an important holiday. Prepare a review for your classmates. Include the name of the movie, an outline of the plot, and a discussion of the way the holiday is presented. Say why you chose this particular movie.

3   Arrangement in Black and White

Dorothy Parker

(1893–1967)

Dorothy Parker was born in New Jersey, but she lived most of her life in New York City, where she wrote for the *New Yorker, Vanity Fair,* and *Vogue*. She helped organize the Algonquin Round Table, a well-known group of artists who met daily for lunch. During the 1930s and 1940s Parker lived in Hollywood. She wrote a number of screenplays and won an Oscar for her work on the film *A Star Is Born* (1937). Because of her left-wing politics, she was later banned from writing for Hollywood movies. Parker also worked as a journalist. When she died, she left everything she owned to civil rights leader Martin Luther King, Jr. Many of Parker's poems and short stories appear in *The Poetry and Short Stories of Dorothy Parker* (1994). Her story "Big Blonde" won the O. Henry Award in 1929.

Arrangement in Black and White

A woman at a party reveals her true feelings about the guest of honor.

"Arrangement in Black and White" was written in 1927, a time when discrimination against African-Americans was both widespread and socially acceptable in much of the United States. In the South, laws kept blacks and whites apart. In the North, where this story takes place, racial prejudice was also common but less openly expressed. At times prejudice was even unconscious. The expressions "Negro" and "colored" were used in more liberal circles to refer to black people. In contrast, the expression "nigger" was and still is a highly offensive term. Today, "African-American" is often used when referring to black Americans.

The woman with the pink velvet poppies twined[1] round the assisted gold of her hair[2] traversed the crowded room at an interesting gait[3] combining a skip with a sidle, and clutched[4] the lean arm of her host.

5   "Now I got you!" she said. "Now you can't get away!"

"Why, hello," said her host. "Well. How are you?"

"Oh, I'm finely[5]," she said. "Just simply finely. Listen. I want you to do me the most terrible favor. Will you? Will you please? Pretty please?"

10   "What is it?" said her host.

"Listen," she said. "I want to meet Walter Williams. Honestly, I'm just simply crazy about[6] that man. Oh, when he sings! When he sings those spirituals![7] Well, I said to Burton, 'It's a good thing for you[8] Walter Williams is colored,' I said, 'or you'd have lots of reason

15 to be jealous.' I'd really love to meet him. I'd like to tell him I've heard him sing. Will you be an angel and introduce me to him?"

"Why, certainly," said her host. "I thought you'd met him. The party's for him. Where is he, anyway?"

"He's over there by the bookcase," she said. "Let's wait till those

20 people get through[9] talking to him. Well, I think you're simply marvelous, giving this perfectly marvelous party for him, and

---

1 **twined** twisted
2 **assisted gold of her hair** hair that has been dyed blonde
3 **gait** way of walking
4 **clutched** held tightly
5 **finely** doing well (unusual usage)

6 **I'm . . . crazy about** I adore
7 **spirituals** religious songs first sung by African-American slaves
8 **it's a good thing for you [that] . . .** you're lucky that . . . (informal)
9 **get through** finish

having him meet all these white people, and all. Isn't he terribly grateful?"

"I hope not," said her host.

25 "I think it's really terribly nice," she said. "I do. I don't see why on earth it isn't perfectly all right to meet colored people. I haven't any feeling at all about it—not one single bit. Burton—oh, he's just the other way. Well, you know, he comes from Virginia, and you know how they are."

30 "Did he come tonight?" said her host.

"No, he couldn't," she said. "I'm a regular grass widow[10] tonight. I told him when I left, 'There's no telling[11] what I'll do,' I said. He was just so tired out, he couldn't move. Isn't it a shame?"

"Ah," said her host.

35 "Wait till I tell him I met Walter Williams!" she said. "He'll just about die. Oh, we have more arguments about colored people. I talk to him like I don't know what, I get so excited. 'Oh, don't be so silly,' I say. But I must say for Burton, he's heaps broader-minded[12] than lots of these Southerners. He's really awfully fond of colored

40 people. Well, he says himself, he wouldn't have white servants. And you know, he had this old colored nurse, this regular old nigger mammy,[13] and he just simply loves her. Why, every time he goes home, he goes out in the kitchen to see her. He does, really, to this day. All he says is, he says he hasn't got a word to say against

45 colored people as long as they keep their place.[14] He's always doing things for them—giving them clothes and I don't know what all. The only thing he says, he says he wouldn't sit down at the table with one for a million dollars. 'Oh,' I say to him, 'you make me sick, talking like that.' I'm just terrible to him. Aren't I terrible?"

50 "Oh, no, no, no," said her host. "No, no."

"I am," she said. "I know I am. Poor Burton! Now, me, I don't feel that way at all. I haven't the slightest feeling about colored people. Why, I'm just crazy about some of them. They're just like children—just as easy-going, and always singing and laughing and

55 everything. Aren't they the happiest things you ever saw in your life? Honestly, it makes me laugh just to hear them. Oh, I like them. I really do. Well, now, listen, I have this colored laundress,[15] I've

---

10 **grass widow** woman whose husband is absent
11 **there's no telling . . .** you can't predict . . .
12 **heaps broader-minded** much more tolerant
13 **mammy** insulting reference to an African-American nanny
14 **keep their place** always act in a way appropriate to their low position (idiom)
15 **laundress** woman who washes clothes for a living

had her for years, and I'm devoted to her. She's a real character.[16] And I want to tell you, I think of her as my friend. That's the way I think of her. As I say to Burton, 'Well, for Heaven's sakes,[17] we're all human beings!' Aren't we?"

"Yes," said her host. "Yes, indeed."

"Now this Walter Williams," she said. "I think a man like that's a real artist. I do. I think he deserves an awful lot of credit.[18] Goodness, I'm so crazy about music or anything, I don't care *what* color he is. I honestly think if a person's an artist, nobody ought to have any feeling at all about meeting them. That's absolutely what I say to Burton. Don't you think I'm right?"

"Yes," said her host. "Oh, yes."

"That's the way I feel," she said. "I just can't understand people being narrow-minded.[19] Why, I absolutely think it's a privilege to meet a man like Walter Williams. Yes, I do. I haven't any feeling at all. Well, my goodness, the good Lord[20] made him, just the same as He did any of us. Didn't He?"

"Surely," said her host. "Yes, indeed."

"That's what I say," she said. "Oh, I get so furious when people are narrow-minded about colored people. It's just all I can do not to say something. Of course, I do admit when you get a bad colored man, they're simply terrible. But as I say to Burton, there are some bad white people, too, in this world. Aren't there?"

"I guess there are," said her host.

"Why, I'd really be glad to have a man like Walter Williams come to my house and sing for us, some time," she said. "Of course, I couldn't ask him on account of[21] Burton, but I wouldn't have any feeling about it at all. Oh, can't he sing! Isn't it marvelous, the way they all have music in them? It just seems to be right *in* them. Come on, let's us go on over and talk to him. Listen, what shall I do when I'm introduced? Ought I to shake hands? Or what?"

"Why, do whatever you want," said her host.

"I guess maybe I'd better," she said. "I wouldn't for the world[22] have him think I had any feeling. I think I'd better shake hands, just the way I would with anybody else. That's just exactly what I'll do."

---

16 **She's a real character.** She's an interesting and unusual person.

17 **for Heaven's sakes** exclamation of impatience or emphasis (usually written as *for heaven's sake*)

18 **he deserves an awful lot of credit** he should be appreciated for his many achievements

19 **narrow-minded** intolerant

20 **the good Lord** God (Christian expression)

21 **on account of** because of

22 **for (all) the world** even if I were given the whole world in exchange (expression used for emphasis)

They reached the tall young Negro, standing by the bookcase. The host performed introductions; the Negro bowed.

95 "How do you do?" he said. "Isn't it a nice party?"

The woman with the pink velvet poppies extended her hand at the length of her arm and held it so, in fine determination,[23] for all the world to see, until the Negro took it, shook it, and gave it back to her.

100 "Oh, how do you do, Mr. Williams," she said. "Well how do you do. I've just been saying, I've enjoyed your singing so awfully much. I've been to your concerts, and we have you on the phonograph[24] and everything. Oh, I just enjoy it!"

She spoke with great distinctness, moving her lips meticulously,[25] 105 as if in parlance with the deaf.[26]

"I'm so glad," he said.

"I'm just simply crazy about that 'Water Boy' thing you sing," she said. "Honestly, I can't get it out of my head. I have my husband nearly crazy, the way I go around humming it all the time. Oh, he 110 looks just as black as the ace of—.[27] Well. Tell me, where on earth do you ever get all those songs of yours? How do you ever get hold of them?"

"Why," he said, "there are so many different—"

"I should think you'd love singing them," she said. "It must be 115 more fun. All those darling old spirituals—oh, I just love them! Well, what are you doing, now? Are you still keeping up[28] your singing? Why don't you have another concert, some time?"

"I'm having one the sixteenth of this month," he said.

"Well, I'll be there," she said. "I'll be there, if I possibly can. You 120 can count on me. Goodness, here comes a whole raft of people[29] to talk to you. You're just a regular guest of honor! Oh, who's that girl in white? I've seen her some place."

"That's Katherine Burke," said her host.

"Good Heavens," she said, "is that Katherine Burke? Why, 125 she looks entirely different off the stage. I thought she was much better-looking. I had no idea she was so terribly dark. Why, she looks almost like—Oh, I think she's a wonderful actress! Don't you think she's a wonderful actress, Mr. Williams? Oh, I think she's marvelous. Don't you?"

---

23 **in fine determination** with a clear purpose (used ironically here)
24 **phonograph** record player
25 **meticulously** slowly and carefully
26 **as if in parlance with the deaf** as if speaking to a person who can't hear
27 **black as the ace of [spades]** a racist expression referring to skin color, which comes from playing cards
28 **keeping up** continuing
29 **a whole raft of people** a lot of people (informal)

130 "Yes, I do," he said.

"Oh, I do, too," she said. "Just wonderful. Well, goodness, we must give someone else a chance to talk to the guest of honor. Now, don't forget, Mr. Williams, I'm going to be at that concert if I possibly can. I'll be there applauding like everything. And if I can't
135 come, I'm going to tell everybody I know to go, anyway. Don't you forget!"

"I won't," he said. "Thank you so much."

The host took her arm and piloted[30] her into the next room.

"Oh, my dear," she said. "I nearly died! Honestly, I give you
140 my word, I nearly passed away. Did you hear that terrible break I made? I was just going to say Katherine Burke looked almost like a nigger. I just caught myself in time. Oh, do you think he noticed?"

"I don't believe so," said her host.

"Well, thank goodness," she said, "because I wouldn't have
145 embarrassed him for anything. Why, he's awfully nice. Just as nice as he can be. Nice manners, and everything. You know, so many colored people, you give them an inch, and they walk all over you.[31] But he doesn't try any of that. Well, he's got more sense, I suppose. He's really nice. Don't you think so?"

150 "Yes," said her host.

"I liked him," she said. "I haven't any feeling at all because he's a colored man. I felt just as natural as I would with anybody. Talked to him just as naturally, and everything. But honestly, I could hardly keep a straight face.[32] I kept thinking of Burton. Oh, wait till I tell
155 Burton I called him 'Mister.'"

---

30 **piloted** led
31 **you give them an inch, and they walk all over you** Usually expressed: *Give them an inch and they'll take a mile.* If you offer those people a small benefit, they will take advantage of you to get more. (a saying)
32 **I could hardly keep a straight face.** It was difficult to stop myself from laughing. (idiom)

FIRST READING

A Thinking About the Story

Discuss the following question with a partner.

> Did you find the woman likeable? Explain your answer.

B Understanding the Plot

Be prepared to answer the following questions with a partner or your class.

1. What event is taking place?
2. Who are the people at the event? List them and explain their roles.
3. Who is Burton? What reason does the speaker give for his absence? Do you think it is the real reason? Explain your answer.
4. What does Burton think about black people? Support your answer with examples from the story.
5. Where is Burton from? How does this help explain his attitude toward black people?
6. Whom does the pronoun *they* refer to in lines 85–86?
7. When she meets Mr. Williams, what does the speaker's body language (lines 96–99) and manner of speech (lines 104–105) tell us about what she is really feeling?
8. What is Burton's reaction when his wife sings Mr. Williams's songs at home?
9. How closely has the woman followed Mr. Williams's career? (lines 114–118) Explain your answer.
10. What prejudiced comment does the woman begin to make when she sees Katherine Burke? (lines 124–127) Do you think Mr. Williams noticed what the woman almost said? Explain your answer.
11. Do you agree with the speaker's statement that she talked "naturally" to Mr. Williams? (line 153) Explain your answer.
12. Why will Burton be amazed that his wife referred to Walter Williams as "Mister"? What does this tell you about Burton's attitude toward race?

PART 2

CRITICAL THINKING

A Exploring Themes

Reread "Arrangement in Black and White." Then answer the following questions, which explore the story more deeply.

1. Underline all the sentences in which the speaker says she doesn't have any "feeling" about black people. What does she mean? Why does she repeat this expression so many times?

2. There are many contradictions between what the speaker claims to think about race and what her attitude really is. List some of these contradictions.

3. The woman stereotypes (makes unfair generalizations about) black people several times. Look at lines 53–56, 78–79, 85–86, and 146–147. Explain how each stereotype shows her prejudice.

4. What does the woman suggest about the special place of artists in society? (lines 63–68)

B Analyzing Style

SATIRE

Satire is the use of humor to criticize the behavior and values of a person or a group. The goal of satire is to draw attention to problems and point out the need for change. Dorothy Parker was well known as a writer of satire. In "Arrangement in Black and White," she makes fun of the speaker's hypocritical attitudes. She suggests that even though many white people didn't think they were prejudiced against blacks, their actions and words indicated the opposite.

For example, when the speaker talks about her husband's affection for his old nanny, she thinks this proves he isn't prejudiced (lines 41–44). However, she doesn't see how offensive it is that he will only visit his old nanny in the kitchen and won't invite her into any other room in the house. Also, by using the racist term *mammy*, she reveals her own prejudice without realizing it.

Exercise 1

With a partner, look at the following quotes from the story. For each quote, first answer the question. Then discuss how the quote is an example of satire.

1. "'It's a good thing for you Walter Williams is colored,' I said, 'or you'd have lots of reason to be jealous.'" (lines 13–15)

   Why is the woman sure her husband wouldn't be jealous?

2. "Well, I think you're simply marvelous, giving this perfectly marvelous party for him, and having him meet all these white people, and all. Isn't he terribly grateful?" (lines 20–23)

    Why does the woman think Walter Williams should be grateful?

3. "Well, he says himself, he wouldn't have white servants." (line 40)

    What does the woman believe this shows about her husband? What does it really show?

4. "Well, now, listen, I have this colored laundress, I've had her for years, and I'm devoted to her. She's a real character. And I want to tell you, I think of her as my friend." (lines 57–59)

    Do you think the woman really thinks of the laundress as her friend? Do you think it's likely that the laundress would call the woman a friend? Explain your answers.

5. "I felt just as natural as I would with anybody. Talked to him just as naturally, and everything." (lines 152–153)

    How does the woman think she talked to Mr. Williams? How did she actually talk to him?

Exercise 2

Find one more quote that may not reflect the woman's true feelings.

DIALOGUE

Dialogue consists of the lines that characters say out loud. Scenes in fiction that contain a lot of dialogue can feel like a play, where the characters act out their roles by speaking to each other.

In "Arrangement in Black and White" there is very little description. Instead, the story consists almost entirely of dialogue spoken by the female guest. Parker chooses to reveal her character's prejudices through what the woman says rather than to comment more directly on her behavior or her words. Almost every time the guest speaks, she shows her prejudice. There is no need for the author to comment.

Parker uses the woman's particular way of speaking to show her personality. Her speech includes excited repetitions and cheerful informality. For example, when she meets the host, she says, *"Listen. I want you to do me the most terrible favor. Will you? Will you please? Pretty please?"* (lines 7–9). Frequently, the woman's speech concludes with a tag question: *". . . there are some bad white people, too, in this world. Aren't there?"* (lines 79–80). These questions reflect her desire for the host's approval.

Answer the following questions.

1. Why does Dorothy Parker choose to end many of the woman's sentences with an exclamation point? How do these exclamation points help us understand the character better?
2. What impression do we get of the woman from the fact that she does almost all the talking?
3. Find at least two examples in the story that capture the conversational tone of the woman's speech.
4. Neither the host nor Mr. Williams speaks much, but when they speak, they reveal something about themselves. What do we learn about them from the few words they say?

C Judging for Yourself

Express yourself as personally as you like in your answers to the following questions.

1. Do you think the woman is less prejudiced than her husband? Explain your answer.
2. In your view, why did the woman go to the party?
3. Do you think the host should have confronted the woman about her comments? Explain your answer.
4. Do you think that the woman's experience meeting Walter Williams at the party will change her beliefs about black people? Explain your answer.

D Making Connections

Answer the following questions in a small group.

1. What stereotypes do outsiders have about your country and its people? Do you agree with any of these stereotypes?
2. Is there discrimination against certain groups of people in your country? If so, which groups? Why do you think people discriminate against them?
3. Are some types of artists better respected than others in your country (for example, actors, writers, painters, dancers, or singers)? Explain your answer.
4. In your culture, when people meet each other for the first time at a party, what do they usually talk about? What subjects are typically avoided?

E Debate

Decide whether you are for or against the following statement. Write several arguments that support your view. Share your points with a classmate who has taken the opposite position.

> Prejudice is part of human nature.

PART 3

GRAMMAR IN CONTEXT

QUOTATION MARKS IN DIALOGUE

Correct punctuation is important for clear writing. In dialogue, **quotation marks** show who is speaking and what is being said. In American English, double quotation marks are used to indicate when a person begins and ends speaking: *"I don't believe so," said her host* (line 143).

- A new indented paragraph begins each time a different speaker starts talking. The punctuation that ends the quote—a comma, period, question mark, or exclamation point—is placed inside the closing quotation mark.

    "Now I got you!" she said. "Now you can't get away!" (line 5)

    "Did he come tonight?" said her host. (line 30)

- When the narrator interrupts a person's speech in mid-sentence with an expression like *he said*, commas are used to separate the two parts of the sentence. The second part of the sentence starts with a lowercase letter.

    "Well, thank goodness," she said, "because I wouldn't have embarrassed him for anything." (lines 144–145)

- When there is a quote within a quote, the inside quote is contained in single quotation marks.

    "'Oh, don't be so silly,' I say." (lines 37–38)

- When a writer quotes a person who cites the title of a poem, song, or other work within that quote, single quotation marks are used to set off the title.

    "I'm just simply crazy about that 'Water Boy' thing you sing," she said. (lines 107–108)

It should be noted that many writers adapt punctuation to suit their style, including some who don't use quotation marks at all. However, you are advised to use standard punctuation rules in your writing.

Look at the following sentences and punctuate them correctly.

1. I'm afraid I have to leave this delightful party he reluctantly told his host

2. Give me his name and address she demanded or I will leave immediately

3. Will he ever allow me to host a black artist she wondered aloud

4. I love that song Water Boy that you recently loaned me she told him enthusiastically

5. We will never discriminate against anyone because of the color of his or her skin he said angrily I simply will not allow it you're fired

6. She asked when are you performing Water Boy next

7. She asked him when he would be performing Water Boy next

8. Can you give me a ride home from the party she asked him it doesn't matter what time you're leaving

9. The host turned to Mr. Williams saying it has been an honor to have you we all look forward to your concert this month

10. Burton you won't believe what I did at the party she exclaimed I actually shook the black artist's hand and addressed him as Mister

---

PART 4 VOCABULARY BUILDING

IDIOMS WITH *KEEP*

Learning **idioms** is an important part of building vocabulary. Idioms can be difficult since their meaning can rarely be understood by looking at or listening to each word. For example, in "Arrangement in Black and White," the woman says that she could hardly *keep a straight face* (line 154), meaning that it was difficult for her not to laugh.

Exercise 1

Look at the following list of idioms that are formed from the verb *keep* and a body part. Match each idiom to its definition. The first one is done for you.

__c__ 1. keep on your toes   **a.** be practical

_____ 2. keep your eye on   **b.** try not to be noticed

_____ 3. keep your chin up   **c.** be ready for anything

_____ 4. keep a cool head   **d.** stay positive

_____ 5. keep your head down   **e.** stay calm

_____ 6. keep your feet on the ground   **f.** maintain a skill

_____ 7. keep your hand in   **g.** watch closely

_____ 8. keep someone at arm's length   **h.** not get too close to someone

Exercise 2

Complete the following sentences with the appropriate idioms from Exercise 1. You may need to change the pronoun. The first one is done for you.

1. Policemen need to _____ *keep on their toes* _____ when they follow a suspect into a building.

2. The politician decided to _____ until the scandal died down.

3. Don't despair. _____ and everything will seem brighter tomorrow morning.

4. Although the musician has retired, he will still _____ _____ by practicing the piano every day.

5. While driving, it is essential to _____ the road at all times.

6. In an emergency, everyone should try to _____.

7. Stop dreaming about becoming a rock star. You need to _____.

8. I don't like my neighbor, so I've decided to _____.

INFORMAL EXPRESSIONS

Since dialogue represents natural speech, it often contains **informal expressions** that are common in spoken English but are not appropriate in formal writing.

Exercise 3

Look at the following informal expressions that appear in the story (with a few minor changes). Work with a partner to figure out what each expression means and how to use it appropriately.

1. Do me a favor. (line 8)
2. I'm just crazy about . . . (line 12)
3. Will you be an angel and . . .? (line 16)
4. She's a real character. (line 58)
5. for Heaven's sake[s] (line 60)
6. I wouldn't for all the world . . . (line 90)
7. Where on earth . . .? (lines 110–111)
8. I nearly died! (line 139)

Exercise 4

With your partner, write a dialogue between two people at a party, using at least four of the expressions listed in Exercise 3. Read your dialogue aloud and share it with another pair of students in your class.

PART 5 WRITING ACTIVITIES

1. Write three paragraphs about a major social injustice in your country. Describe the problem and explain its background. Conclude by saying what you think should be done to change the situation.

2. Imagine you are at a party and are introduced to the guest of honor, a celebrity you're excited to meet. Write a dialogue of your conversation with him or her. Punctuate your dialogue correctly, paying special attention to the rules governing quotation marks. Try to make your dialogue sound as natural as possible.

3. Dorothy Parker wrote many short stories. Find another one of her short stories online or in a library. Write a review in which you discuss the story's plot, themes, and style. Discuss any similarities between your story and "Arrangement in Black and White." Say whether you recommend the story and why.

4 A Serious Talk

Raymond Carver

(1938–1988)

Raymond Carver was born in the Pacific Northwest to working-class parents. As a young man he moved to California, where he began his writing career. Carver is famous for his short stories dealing with the difficult lives of working-class characters. His writing is characterized by dark themes relieved by surprising moments of humor. His plain writing style without much description has often been compared to Ernest Hemingway's. Like Hemingway, Carver suffered from alcoholism, which he overcame only late in life. Carver's collection of stories *Will You Please Be Quiet, Please?* (1976) established his reputation. Another collection, *Where I'm Calling From* (1989), was published after his death. Carver also wrote several collections of poetry, including *Where Water Comes Together with Other Water* (1985) and *Ultramarine* (1986). He won five O. Henry awards for his short stories.

A Serious Talk

A man has a difficult time accepting what has happened to his marriage.

Vera's car was there, no others, and Burt gave thanks for that. He pulled into the drive and stopped beside the pie he'd dropped the night before. It was still there, the aluminum pan upside down, a halo of pumpkin filling[1] on the pavement. It was the day after Christmas.

He'd come on Christmas day to visit his wife and children. Vera had warned him beforehand. She'd told him the score.[2] She'd said he had to be out by six o'clock because her friend and his children were coming for dinner.

They had sat in the living room and solemnly opened the presents Burt had brought over. They had opened his packages while other packages wrapped in festive paper lay piled under the tree waiting for after six o'clock.

He had watched the children open their gifts, waited while Vera undid the ribbon on hers. He saw her slip off the paper, lift the lid, take out the cashmere[3] sweater.

"It's nice," she said. "Thank you, Burt."

"Try it on," his daughter said.

"Put it on," his son said.

Burt looked at his son, grateful for his backing him up.[4]

She did try it on. Vera went into the bedroom and came out with it on.

"It's nice," she said.

"It's nice on *you*," Burt said, and felt a welling in his chest.[5]

He opened his gifts. From Vera, a gift certificate at Sondheim's men's store. From his daughter, a matching comb and brush. From his son, a ballpoint pen.

Vera served sodas, and they did a little talking. But mostly they looked at the tree. Then his daughter got up and began setting the dining-room table,[6] and his son went off to his room.

---

1 **halo of pumpkin filling** the inside of a pie, which looks like a ring of light (figurative language suggesting an angel's head)
2 **She'd told him the score.** She'd told him the unpleasant truth. (idiom)
3 **cashmere** an expensive, soft wool

4 **backing him up** supporting him
5 **a welling in his chest** an emotion rising from deep inside him
6 **setting the dining-room table** getting the table ready for a meal

But Burt liked it where he was. He liked it in front of the fireplace, a glass in his hand, his house, his home.

Then Vera went into the kitchen.

From time to time his daughter walked into the dining room with something for the table. Burt watched her. He watched her fold the linen napkins into the wine glasses. He watched her put a slender vase in the middle of the table. He watched her lower a flower into the vase, doing it ever so carefully.

A small wax and sawdust log burned on the grate.[7] A carton of five more sat ready on the hearth.[8] He got up from the sofa and put them all in the fireplace. He watched until they flamed. Then he finished his soda and made for the patio door. On the way, he saw the pies lined up on the sideboard. He stacked[9] them in his arms, all six, one for every ten times she had ever betrayed him.

In the driveway in the dark, he'd let one fall as he fumbled with[10] the door.

The front door was permanently locked since the night his key had broken off inside it. He went around to the back. There was a wreath[11] on the patio door. He rapped on the glass. Vera was in her bathrobe. She looked out at him and frowned. She opened the door a little.

Burt said, "I want to apologize to you for last night. I want to apologize to the kids, too."

Vera said, "They're not here."

She stood in the doorway and he stood on the patio next to the philodendron plant. He pulled at some lint on his sleeve.

She said, "I can't take any more.[12] You tried to burn the house down."

"I did not."

"You did. Everybody here was a witness."

He said, "Can I come in and talk about it?"

She drew the robe together at her throat and moved back inside.

She said, "I have to go somewhere in an hour."

He looked around. The tree blinked on and off.[13] There was a pile of colored tissue paper and shiny boxes at one end of the sofa.

---

7 **grate** metal bars at the bottom of a fireplace
8 **hearth** area in front of a fireplace
9 **stacked** placed one on top of another
10 **fumbled with** tried with difficulty to open
11 **wreath** ring of flowers or leaves, usually hung around Christmas

12 **I can't take any more.** I can't endure this any longer. (idiom)
13 **The tree blinked on and off.** The electric lights of the Christmas tree flashed.

A turkey carcass[14] sat on a platter in the center of the dining-room table, the leathery remains in a bed of parsley as if in a horrible nest. A cone of ash filled the fireplace. There were some empty Shasta cola cans in there too. A trail of smoke stains rose up to the bricks
70 to the mantel,[15] where the wood that stopped them was scorched[16] black.

He turned around and went back to the kitchen.

He said, "What time did your friend leave last night?"

She said, "If you're going to start that, you can go right now."

75 He pulled a chair out and sat down at the kitchen table in front of the big ashtray. He closed his eyes and opened them. He moved the curtain aside and looked out at the backyard. He saw a bicycle without a front wheel standing upside down. He saw weeds growing along the redwood fence.

80 She ran water into a saucepan. "Do you remember Thanksgiving?" she said. "I said then that was the last holiday you were going to wreck[17] for us. Eating bacon and eggs instead of turkey at ten o'clock at night."

"I know it," he said. "I said I'm sorry."

85 "Sorry isn't good enough."

The pilot light[18] was out again. She was at the stove trying to get the gas going under the pan of water.

"Don't burn yourself," he said. "Don't catch yourself on fire."

He considered her robe catching fire, him jumping up from the
90 table, throwing her down onto the floor and rolling her over and over into the living room, where he would cover her with his body. Or should he run to the bedroom for a blanket?

"Vera?"

She looked at him.

95 "Do you have anything to drink? I could use a drink this morning."

"There's some vodka in the freezer."

"When did you start keeping vodka in the freezer?"

"Don't ask."

100 "Okay," he said, "I won't ask."

He got out the vodka and poured some into a cup he found on the counter.

---

14 **turkey carcass** the leftover parts of a cooked turkey
15 **mantel** shelf above a fireplace
16 **scorched** burnt on the surface
17 **wreck** destroy
18 **pilot light** small flame used to light a gas stove

She said, "Are you just going to drink it like that, out of a cup?"
She said, "Jesus, Burt. What'd you want to talk about, anyway?
105 I told you I have someplace to go. I have a flute lesson at one
o'clock."

"Are you still taking flute?"[19]

"I just said so. What is it? Tell me what's on your mind,[20] and
then I have to get ready."

110 "I wanted to say I was sorry."

She said, "You said that."

He said, "If you have any juice, I'll mix it with this vodka."

She opened the refrigerator and moved things around.

"There's cranapple juice," she said.

115 "That's fine," he said.

"I'm going to the bathroom," she said.

He drank the cup of cranapple juice and vodka. He lit a cigarette
and tossed the match into the big ashtray that always sat on the
kitchen table. He studied the butts[21] in it. Some of them were
120 Vera's brand, and some of them weren't. Some even were lavender-
colored. He got up and dumped[22] it all under the sink.

The ashtray was not really an ashtray. It was a big dish of
stoneware they'd bought from a bearded potter on the mall in Santa
Clara. He rinsed it out and dried it. He put it back on the table. And
125 then he ground out his cigarette[23] in it.

The water on the stove began to bubble just as the phone began
to ring.

He heard her open the bathroom door and call to him through
the living room. "Answer that! I'm about to[24] get into the shower."

130 The kitchen phone was on the counter in a corner behind the
roasting pan. He moved the roasting pan and picked up the receiver.

"Is Charlie there?" the voice said.

"No," Burt said.

"Okay," the voice said.

135 While he was seeing to[25] the coffee, the phone rang again.

"Charlie?"

"Not here," Burt said.

This time he left the receiver off the hook.[26]

---

19 **taking flute** having flute lessons (idiom)
20 **on your mind** bothering you (idiom)
21 **butts** cigarette ends
22 **dumped** carelessly threw
23 **ground out his cigarette** put out his cigarette

24 **about to** going to do something very soon
25 **was seeing to** was dealing with
26 **he left the receiver off the hook** he didn't put the telephone back on its holder

Vera came back into the kitchen wearing jeans and a sweater and brushing her hair.

140 He spooned the instant[27] into the cups of hot water and then spilled some vodka into his. He carried the cups over to the table.

She picked up the receiver, listened. She said, "What's this? Who was on the phone?"

145 "Nobody," he said. "Who smokes colored cigarettes?"

"I do."

"I didn't know you did that."

"Well, I do."

She sat across from him and drank her coffee. They smoked and 150 used the ashtray.

There were things he wanted to say, grieving things, consoling things,[28] things like that.

"I'm smoking three packs a day," Vera said. "I mean, if you really want to know what goes on around here."

155 "God almighty," Burt said.

Vera nodded.

"I didn't come over here to hear that," he said.

"What did you come over here to hear, then? You want to hear the house burned down?"

160 "Vera," he said. "It's Christmas. That's why I came."

"It's the day after Christmas," she said. "Christmas has come and gone," she said. "I don't ever want to see another one."

"What about me?" he said. "You think I look forward to[29] holidays?"

165 The phone rang again. Burt picked it up.

"It's someone wanting Charlie," he said.

"What?"

"Charlie," Burt said.

Vera took the phone. She kept her back to him as she talked. 170 Then she turned to him and said, "I'll take this call in the bedroom. So would you please hang up[30] after I've picked it up in there? I can tell, so hang it up when I say."

He took the receiver. She left the kitchen. He held the receiver to his ear and listened. He heard nothing. Then he heard a man 175 clear his throat.[31] Then he heard Vera pick up the other phone. She shouted, "Okay, Burt! I have it now, Burt!"

---

27 **the instant** powdered coffee that can be made quickly

28 **grieving things, consoling things** sad and comforting words

29 **look forward to** eagerly await

30 **hang up** put the phone down

31 **clear his throat** cough once to make it easier to speak

He put down the receiver and stood looking at it. He opened the silverware drawer and pushed things around inside. He opened another drawer. He looked in the sink. He went into the dining

180 room and got the carving knife.[32] He held it under hot water until the grease broke and ran off. He wiped the blade on his sleeve. He moved to the phone, doubled the cord, and sawed through without any trouble at all. He examined the ends of the cord. Then he shoved the phone back into its corner behind the roasting pan.

185 She came in. She said, "The phone went dead. Did you do anything to the telephone?" She looked at the phone and then picked it up from the counter.

"Son of a bitch!" she screamed. She screamed, "Out, out, where you belong!" She was shaking the phone at him. "That's it! I'm

190 going to get a restraining order,[33] that's what I'm going to get!"

The phone made a *ding* when she banged it down on the counter.

"I'm going next door to call the police if you don't get out of here now!"

195 He picked up the ashtray. He held it by its edge. He posed with it like a man preparing to hurl a discus.[34]

"Please," she said. "That's our ashtray."

He left through the patio door. He was not certain, but he thought he had proved something. He hoped he had made

200 something clear. The thing was, they had to have a serious talk soon. There were things that needed talking about, important things that had to be discussed. They'd talk again. Maybe after the holidays were over and things got back to normal. He'd tell her the goddamn ashtray was a goddamn dish, for example.

205 He stepped around the pie in the driveway and got back into his car. He started the car and put it into reverse. It was hard managing until he put the ashtray down.

---

32 **carving knife** large knife with a sharp blade for slicing meat

33 **restraining order** legal paper forbidding one person from making contact with another

34 **hurl a discus** throw a heavy disc in an athletic competition

FIRST READING

A Thinking About the Story

Discuss the following question with a partner.

Why do you think Burt and Vera separated?

B Understanding the Plot

Be prepared to answer the following questions with a partner or your class.

1. On what two days does the story take place?
2. On the first day, why does Vera say that Burt needs to leave the house by six o'clock?
3. How is Burt's gift to Vera different from Vera's gift to Burt?
4. How many pies does Burt take? What happens to them?
5. What do we learn happened to Burt's house key?
6. On the second day, why does Burt want to apologize to Vera and the children?
7. Why does Burt ask what time Vera's friend left? How does Vera respond to his question?
8. What other holiday does Vera accuse Burt of spoiling? What happened then?
9. Why is Burt so interested in the cigarette butts in the ashtray? (lines 119–121)
10. Who do you think is calling on the telephone? Why does the caller ask to speak to "Charlie"?
11. Why does Burt leave the receiver off the hook? (line 138)
12. Why does Vera not want Burt to hear the telephone conversation?
13. What is Burt looking for in the kitchen? What does he do with the object when he finds it?
14. What does Burt take from the house at the end? Why does he choose this particular object?
15. Does Burt succeed in having a serious talk with Vera?

PART 2

CRITICAL THINKING

A Exploring Themes

Reread "A Serious Talk." Then answer the following questions, which explore the story more deeply.

1. Why is holiday time so emotionally difficult for Burt?

2. Discuss Burt's desire to have a serious talk with Vera. What do you think he wants to say to her? Does he have a realistic picture of their future together?

3. How would you describe Burt's personality? In your answer, consider how he reacts to situations that upset him. Give examples.

4. In lines 86–92, Burt is concerned for Vera and imagines rescuing her from a fire. What does this fantasy of rescuing Vera show us about Burt?

B Analyzing Style

MINIMALISM

Raymond Carver is known for his **minimalist** writing style, meaning that he uses very little descriptive language. He doesn't directly tell us what is going on inside the minds of his characters. Instead, he reveals his characters' thoughts and feelings through what they say and do. Although minimalist writing may appear to be simple, its effect can be powerful and complex.

Minimalism demands careful reading. In order to understand the characters and their motivations, we have to use **inference**. Inference means figuring out additional facts from limited information. By using inference, we reach a more complete understanding of the story.

Exercise

Answer the following questions.

1. What can we infer about Vera's relationship with her *friend*? (lines 7–9) Explain your answer.

2. What can we infer about the children's feelings toward their parents in the scene where Christmas presents are exchanged?

3. What is suggested about Burt's state of mind in lines 24 and 31–32? Find at least one more place where the author reveals Burt's feelings indirectly.

4. Why does Vera *draw her robe together at her throat*? (line 62) What does it tell us about her feelings at that moment?

5. Why does Burt wash the ashtray before grinding out his cigarette in it? (lines 124–125)
6. Why does Burt wash the kitchen knife? (lines 180–181)
7. What do we learn about Vera from her habit of smoking three packs of cigarettes a day?
8. What is suggested about Burt's drinking habits? Give examples from the story.
9. Is Vera a good housekeeper? Give examples from the story.

C Judging for Yourself

Express yourself as personally as you like in your answers to the following questions.

1. Do you think Vera should take Burt back? Explain your answer.
2. Can you sympathize with Burt's actions and feelings? Explain your answer.
3. In your opinion, does Vera handle her two meetings with Burt well? Give reasons for your answer.

D Making Connections

Answer the following questions in a small group.

1. What is the divorce rate in your country? What are the major factors contributing to divorce? Are the rules different depending on whether the person seeking divorce is a man or a woman?
2. In your culture, do couples get counseling if their marriage is in trouble? To whom would they turn for help: a family member, a professional counselor, a religious leader, a respected elder, anyone else?
3. When couples separate in your country, what usually happens to the children?
4. Is the rate of cigarette smoking increasing or decreasing in your country? Which groups of people smoke the most? Explain your answers.

E Debate

Decide whether you are for or against the following statement. Write several arguments that support your view. Share your points with a classmate who has taken the opposite position.

Parents should stay together for the good of their children.

PART 3

GERUNDS AND INFINITIVES

Gerunds and **infinitives** are related to verbs, but they do not function as verbs. The gerund acts as a noun; it is generally formed by adding *–ing* to the base form of a verb. The infinitive can act as a noun, an adjective, or an adverb; it is formed by placing *to* before the base form of a verb.

Rules that govern **gerunds**:

- Gerunds can be the subject or object of a verb or the object of a preposition.

    Eating is essential to life. (subject)

    When did you start smoking? (object)

    Burt and Vera were tired of arguing. (object of a preposition)

- Gerunds can form gerund phrases, which act in the same way as gerunds by themselves.

    Taking the ashtray didn't make Burt feel any better. (subject)

    Some people use heavy drinking to avoid reality. (object)

    Burt looked at his son, grateful for his backing him up. (line 20) (object of a preposition)

- Do not confuse gerunds with present participles, which also end in *–ing* but act as adjectives.

    He saw weeds growing along the redwood fence. (lines 78–79) (present participle)

    Growing flowers is difficult in a garden full of weeds. (gerund)

    For practice with participles, see pages 19–21.

- Certain verbs are followed by a gerund. These include: *admit (to), avoid, consider, delay, enjoy, finish, imagine, keep on, postpone, recommend, suggest,* and *think about.*

    He admitted to setting the house on fire.

    She delayed getting a divorce.

    They sometimes thought about going to a marriage counselor.

Rules that govern **infinitives**:

- When functioning as a noun, an infinitive or infinitive phrase can be the subject or object of a verb, but not the object of a preposition.

    To run a marathon requires a lot of practice. (subject)

    The water on the stove began to bubble. (line 126) (object)

    You tried to burn the house down. (lines 57–58) (object)

- Infinitives are used after the verb *to be* + an adjective.

  *It is impossible **to change your mind**.*

  *I am ready **to leave**.*

- Like adverbs, infinitives can give more information about where, when, or why something happens.

  *She flew home **to see her parents**.*

- Like adjectives, infinitives can give more information about a noun or pronoun.

  *Bring a book **to read** while you wait for your appointment.*

- Certain verbs are followed by an infinitive. These include: *appear, ask, deserve, expect, fail, hesitate, intend, learn, need, offer, plan,* and *want*.

  *You deserve **to have** a happier life.*

  *I fail **to understand** your actions.*

  *Mom wants you **to set** the table for dinner.*

Some common verbs, including *begin, continue, hate, like, love, prefer, propose, start,* and *try*, can be followed by either the gerund or the infinitive.

  *I like **playing** the flute.*

  *I like **to play** the flute.*

Exercise 1

Complete each of the following sentences with either the gerund or the infinitive form of the verb in parentheses. Indicate where both choices are possible.

1. Her mother recommended _____ vitamin pills every day. (take)

2. It started _____ early this morning. (rain)

3. They expect _____ first prize in the competition. (win)

4. I love _____ in the winter. (ski)

5. It is impossible _____ without effort. (succeed)

6. My friend's brother won't admit to _____ the ballet. (like)

7. I would prefer _____ home this weekend. (stay)

8. Are you planning _____ this summer? (travel)

9. You must think about _____ to college. (go)

10. The politician failed _____ the election. (win)

11. It continued _____ for three days in a row. (rain)

12. Consider _____ for extra lessons in math. (go)

13. He hated _____ his favorite singer's concert. (miss)

14. You deserve _____ another chance. (get)

15. On hearing the explanation, he went from _____ sympathetic to hostile. (be)

Exercise 2

Complete the following sentences with either a gerund phrase or an infinitive phrase.

1. Mary enjoys _____.

2. They hope _____.

3. My father deserves _____.

4. Their neighbors seem _____.

5. The student couldn't imagine _____.

6. We tried _____.

7. I needed _____.

8. The nurse offers _____.

9. The rescuers kept on _____.

10. The president proposes _____.

Exercise 3

Find three examples each of gerunds and infinitives in "A Serious Talk." Write sentences using your examples.

PART 4 | # VOCABULARY BUILDING

PHRASAL VERBS

A **phrasal verb** consists of a verb and one or more particles. A particle may be a preposition or an adverb. When the verb and the particle are combined in a phrasal verb, they often mean something very different from their individual parts. Since phrasal verbs are common in English, they are an important part of vocabulary learning.

> *Burt looked at his son, grateful for his **backing** him **up**.* (line 20)

Here, the phrasal verb *back up* means "support." This meaning cannot be determined from the verb *back*.

- Verbs that take an object are called *transitive*. With some transitive phrasal verbs, the particle can be separated from the verb and placed after the object.

    *He **tried on** the sweater.*

    *He **tried** the sweater **on**.*

- If the object of a phrasal verb is a pronoun, the pronoun usually goes between the verb and the particle.

    *He **tried** it **on**.*

    However, with certain transitive phrasal verbs the particle cannot be separated from the verb.

    *He never **got over** his anger.*

    *He never **got over** it.*

- Some phrasal verbs are *intransitive*, meaning that they cannot take an object.

    *His wife didn't want him **to come in**.*

Exercise 1

Look at the following list of phrasal verbs. All of them are used in the story. Write the definition for each in the space provided.

1. get up (line 29)   _____
2. make for (line 42)   _____
3. get out (line 101)   _____
4. put back (line 124)   _____
5. pick up (line 131)   _____
6. go on (line 154)   _____
7. hang up (lines 171–172)   _____
8. get out of (line 193)   _____
9. get back (line 203)   _____

Exercise 2

Complete the sentences that follow with a phrasal verb from Exercise 1. You may need to change the verb form.

1. _____ that cashmere sweater. I am not going to buy it.

2. Parents usually want to know what _____ at home when they leave their children behind.

3. Unfortunately, they were unable to _____ from their vacation in time for their friend's wedding.

4. When the fire alarm rang in the theater, everyone immediately _____ the exit.

5. I can't _____ the telephone now. I'm in the middle of cooking.

6. You should all _____ the house immediately. I can smell gas.

7. The spectators _____ and cheered when their team got a goal.

8. The salesman _____ his best goods to show the rich customer.

9. It is rude to listen to someone's private telephone conversation. You should _____ now.

WRITING ACTIVITIES

1. "A Serious Talk" is told from Burt's point of view. Create a journal entry written by Vera on the night after Christmas. Write down her version of the events that took place over the holiday.

2. Think of a celebration in your life that went wrong. Describe the scene and discuss your feelings about what happened. Try to include both gerunds and infinitives in your explanation.

3. Like Raymond Carver's stories, some television shows in the United States center on working-class families. One example is *Shameless*, a comedy/drama that features an alcoholic father and his numerous children. While the father concentrates on dishonest schemes for making money, his oldest daughter struggles to keep the family together. Choose a television series or movie you've seen that concentrates on the lives of working-class people. Describe the plot, and say what you learned about the lives of the characters.

MOMENTS OF DISCOVERY

Damn Irene
Blackberries
Mr. Lupescu
Niña

5   Damn Irene

Susan O'Neill
(b. 1947)

Susan O'Neill was born in Indiana. She joined the army while studying to be a nurse and was sent to Vietnam. She treated wounded soldiers there from 1969 to 1970. O'Neill wrote a collection of short stories, *Don't Mean Nothing: Short Stories of Vietnam* (2001), based on her experiences. The book, which, unusually, views war from a female perspective, combines seriousness with black humor. From 1973 to 1974 she and her husband, a doctor, were Peace Corps volunteers in Venezuela. O'Neill has also worked as a waitress, singer, reporter, and photographer. She has served as co-editor of *Vestal Review*, a magazine that publishes very short stories. O'Neill has been named a notable author by *Best American Authors*.

Damn Irene

A couple's boating trip ends in an unexpected way.

Harry dipped his paddle blade, the handle at chest level as Toni the Leader had taught them. Just beyond the three kayaks[1] crouched a damp roll of fog; if he reached out, he could've grabbed a handful.

5   "We'll make for[2] Burnt Island," Toni called. "It's getting murky[3]—stick together, we won't get lost."

"Okay," Harry shouted. In the rear seat, Irene said nothing. He glanced back; she paddled clumsily,[4] her face expressionless above her life vest. A wave tossed up spray. He shivered. Cold; he'd hate
10   to have to swim in this bay.

"Left," Toni called. "Follow me."

Harry leaned into the paddle, dipping, dipping, but the kayak did not turn. Fog tickled his arm. "Left, Irene," he ordered. "Push the left pedal."

15   Behind him, her meek[5] voice: "I can't, Honey. It's stuck. The rudder[6] won't go left."

"You're not trying," he said through clenched teeth.[7] Damn Irene. She never tried. She'd seemed so eager to please last year when they were dating. Then he'd married her. What a mistake.

20   She never complained, per se.[8] But when he tried to teach her tennis—coached her, drilled, cajoled,[9] rewarded, bullied, shamed her—she refused to hit the ball right. At last, he joined a club and left her to putter[10] in her silly garden.

He bought her a bike. She didn't bother to keep up with him,
25   and still she strained her knee.

Golf? She lost the balls. Camping? She got poison ivy.[11] And when he took her hunting, she tripped and nearly shot him ("Oops; sorry, honey," she'd said).

Ron and Marcie's kayak shimmered off to the left and dissolved
30   in the mist. Marcie, now—*there* was a game woman.[12] Damn Irene. "Push your left pedal. *Push.*"

---

1   **kayaks** light, narrow boats for one or two people
2   **make for** go toward
3   **murky** dark and foggy
4   **clumsily** without skill
5   **meek** mild and obedient
6   **rudder** underwater part that turns the boat
7   **clenched teeth** teeth closed very tightly

8   **per se** exactly (Latin phrase used to suggest that a contrasting statement will follow)
9   **cajoled** persuaded by means of promises and praise
10 **putter** work without much purpose or focus
11 **poison ivy** a plant that stings and gives a rash when touched
12 **a game woman** a woman ready to try anything

"I am, Honey."

His neck hairs bristled.[13] "You're not."

"I told you, the right pedal works—"

He heard the rustle of the spray skirt[14] that stretched from her waist to the rim of her compartment; the kayak lumbered rightward.[15]

"—but not the left."

"Irene, straighten us out," he commanded.

"I can't, Honey. Honest. My left pedal's broke."

Her wimpy[16] tone set his teeth on edge.[17] "Damn, Irene." He twisted, heard the dip-dip of her paddle, but she was lost in fog.

"Turn this kayak left. *Now.*"

Silence.

Then, softly, tentatively: "Turn it yourself." Dip-dip. "Honey."

His eyes widened. Far away, a buoy gonged.[18]

He slammed the paddle down on the fiberglass hull. "What'd you say?" His heart hammered. He jutted his jaw.[19] *"What??* I'll be damned if I'll paddle for two."[20]

"This wasn't my idea." Her disembodied voice[21] sounded surprised: "You know, it's never my idea."

He heard the snap of a spray skirt pulling free. A splash. A gasp—*Whoo!* The kayak bucked, rolled over; grey water grabbed up for him. Cold. He heard arm-strokes, surprisingly strong, receding, fading, gone. His face bobbed under, up; his paddle knocked the hull, dodged his shivering fingers, floated away.

"Damn, Irene!" Up; under. *"Ireeb?!?"*

But there was only the far-off gong of the buoy.

---

13 **bristled** stood up in anger
14 **spray skirt** removable part of a kayak that prevents the rower from getting wet
15 **lumbered rightward** moved right with difficulty
16 **wimpy** weak, cowardly (slang)
17 **set his teeth on edge** irritated him

18 **a buoy gonged** a safety marker in the water made a loud sound
19 **jutted his jaw** pushed out his chin in anger
20 **I'll be damned if I'll paddle for two.** I refuse to do the work of two people. (expression used to emphasize a negative feeling)
21 **disembodied voice** voice that doesn't seem to come from a person's body

A   Thinking About the Story

Discuss the following question with a partner.

Did you feel more sympathetic toward Harry or Irene? Explain your answer.

B   Understanding the Plot

Be prepared to answer the following questions with a partner or your class.

1. Were Harry and Irene experienced kayakers? Explain your answer.
2. Who is in each of the three kayaks?
3. Why does the fog pose a danger? Give several reasons.
4. How does Harry react when he thinks about swimming in the cold bay? (lines 9–10)
5. What problem does Harry and Irene's kayak develop?
6. About how long have Harry and Irene been married?
7. What methods did Harry use to teach Irene tennis? Did any of them succeed?
8. What other outdoor activities did Harry want Irene to try? What did Irene prefer doing?
9. What does Harry think about Marcie?
10. Why does Irene's voice seem to be *disembodied*? (line 50)
11. Why does Irene free herself from the spray skirt? (lines 52–53)
12. Which physical activity is Irene good at? How do we know?
13. What happens to Harry at the end?

PART 2   CRITICAL THINKING

A   Exploring Themes

Reread "Damn Irene." Then answer the following questions, which explore the story more deeply.

1. If you could give the story a new title that reflects Irene's point of view, what would you call it?
2. How would you describe Harry and Irene's marriage? Explain your answer as fully as possible.

3. At which point in the story does Irene take control of the situation? How does she start acting differently?

4. The ending of "Damn Irene" can be seen as either humorous or unexpectedly dark. Explain how you saw the ending, and justify your interpretation.

B Analyzing Style

PERSONIFICATION

Personification is a figure of speech in which things or abstract ideas are given human characteristics. For example: *Just beyond the three kayaks crouched a damp roll of fog* (lines 2–3). In this example, the fog is described as bending low to the ground, ready to attack. The image of the fog waiting to surround the kayakers creates an atmosphere of danger and helps us predict from the start that the day may end badly.

Exercise 1

Find examples of personification in line 13 and in lines 53–54.

Exercise 2

Explain the personification in each of the following sentences. The first one is done for you.

1. The small kayak protested as the couple climbed in.

    The kayak is compared to a person who is complaining about the weight.

2. The boat's engine sang loudly as it passed the kayakers in the bay.

3. Fear gripped Harry's throat as he struggled to stay above water.

4. Harry could barely see the whispering trees through the thick fog.

5. The setting sun abandoned Harry as he fought to stay above the water.

6. When she left the harbor, the rescue ship had all her crew on deck.

Exercise 3

Write three sentences of your own that are related to the events of the story. Use personification in each sentence.

CHARACTERIZATION

Characterization refers to how an author paints a picture of the people in a story. Sometimes we learn about characters directly through descriptions of their appearance, thoughts, and personality. Other times an author will prefer to "show" rather than "tell," depicting the characters more indirectly. We must then interpret the words and actions of the characters in order to understand their thoughts, feelings, and motivations.

There isn't much description in "Damn Irene." Nevertheless, we get a good sense of the personalities of the two main characters from the way they talk to each other and from Irene's silences. We are also given some of Harry's thoughts. For example: *She'd seemed so eager to please last year when they were dating. Then he'd married her. What a mistake* (lines 18–19). Here, Harry reveals his bitterness and regret about marrying Irene. Although his thoughts are focused on his wife, he is really showing us more about himself.

Exercise 4

Answer the following questions with a partner.

1. Line 21 and lines 46–48 contain many colorful verbs. How do these verbs help paint a picture of Harry? Can you find any other verbs in the story that convey Harry's personality?
2. Irene frequently says "Honey" when she speaks to Harry. How does the way she uses this word change during the story?
3. Harry repeats a certain phrase several times in the story. What is it? What does it indicate about how he views his wife?
4. There are not many adjectives in the story. Pick out a few that help us picture the couple.
5. "Damn Irene" is told through Harry's eyes. What does he fail to see about his wife? How does this contribute to what happens?

C Judging for Yourself

Express yourself as personally as you like in your answers to the following questions.

1. Do you think Irene considers the consequences of her actions at the end of the story?
2. Do you think that Harry deserves what happens to him?
3. Do you think that Irene has tried hard enough to share Harry's hobbies?
4. Do you think Harry would have had a happier marriage if he had married a woman like Marcie?

D Making Connections

Answer the following questions in a small group.

1. Is there a difference in your culture between how people treat each other before and after they get married?

2. Bullying can be verbal or physical. In your society, are men or women more often the victim of bullying? Does it make a difference whether it is verbal or physical?

3. Is it considered important in your culture for a married couple to share hobbies? Explain your answer.

4. Which outdoor sports are popular in your country? Are they the same for men and women?

E Debate

Decide whether you are for or against the following statement. Write several arguments that support your view. Share your points with a classmate who has taken the opposite position.

> It is never justified to lose one's self-control.

PART 3 **GRAMMAR IN CONTEXT**

CONTRACTIONS

A **contraction** occurs when two or more words are shortened into a single word by dropping a letter or letters. The missing letters are indicated by an apostrophe. Contractions are used frequently in spoken English, but they are not usually appropriate in formal writing. In "Damn Irene," most of the story is dialogue, and the author uses many contractions to make the speech sound more natural.

- Subject pronouns can be contracted with the verbs *to be* and *to have*.

    "***It's** getting murky—stick together.*" (lines 5–6) [it is]

    "***We'll** make for Burnt Island,*" Toni called. (line 5) [we will]

    ***He'd** been in the water for an hour before anyone knew he was in trouble.* [he had]

    ***They've** lost sight of the island.* [they have]

    "***That's** a great idea!*" [that is]

- The word *not* is frequently contracted when it comes after a modal or after the verb *to be*.

    "We **won't** get lost." (line 6) [will not]

    "You **shouldn't** be so careless in the fog." [should not]

    You **can't** survive underwater for long. [cannot]

    "**Isn't** it time to return?" [is not]

- Questions with the verbs *to be*, *to do*, and *to have* are frequently contracted.

    "**How's** the weather by the bay?" [how is]

    "**When's** our next kayak lesson?" [when is]

    "**Where'd** Harry go?" [where did]

    "**Who's** got an extra paddle?" [who has]

- The modals *could*, *should*, *would*, and *must* can be contracted with *have*.

    Irene **could've** helped Harry, but she was too angry to care. [could have]

- A noun subject plus the verb *to be* can be contracted.

    The **policeman's** suspicious of the circumstances surrounding Harry's death. [policeman is]

- *Let us* is almost always contracted.

    "**Let's** go sailing today."

Exercise 1

Look at the following sentences from the story. Find the contractions and rewrite them as full forms.

1. If he reached out, he could've grabbed a handful of fog. (adapted from lines 3–4) _____

2. He'd hate to have to swim in this bay. (lines 9–10)
   _____

3. "It's stuck. The rudder won't go left." (lines 15–16)
   _____ , _____

4. "You're not trying." (line 17) _____

5. She'd seemed so eager to please last year when they were dating. (lines 18–19) _____

6. She didn't bother to keep up with him. (line 24)
   _____

7. "What'd you say? I'll be damned if I'll paddle for two." (lines 47–49)
   _____ , _____

Exercise 2

Look at the following sentences written in formal English. Rewrite the sentences using contractions wherever possible.

1. I am so sorry to miss your party. I would go, but my final exam is tomorrow.
2. Who is coming to dinner? Do you not have all the answers to our invitations?
3. The doctor is ready for you now. Please do not continue reading the magazine.
4. Let us go for lunch now. We have worked long enough.
5. It is easy to waste a lot of time on YouTube. My roommate has not stopped watching videos all weekend.
6. How is your class going? I know that it would be very difficult for me to learn engineering.
7. They are really sorry for what they did. They should have sent their apologies sooner.
8. When is the next bus coming? I cannot wait much longer. I will have to take a taxi.
9. Our plane had not taken off yet when a problem was found in the engine.
10. The students must have finished their exams by now. That clock is never late.

MISTAKES WITH CONTRACTIONS

Certain contractions are often used incorrectly. For example, it is easy to confuse *it's/its, who's/whose, they're/their/there,* and *you're/your.*

> **It's** *a foggy day for kayaking.* [it is]
>
> *The kayak rolled onto **its** side.* [possessive]

> *I don't know **who's** coming sailing with us today.* [who is]
>
> *The policeman asked **whose** boat was in the accident.* [possessive]

> **They're** *back from **their** trip to the island.* [they are/possessive]
>
> **Their** *luggage was unfortunately left behind **there**.* [possessive/adverb]

> **You're** *not very happy in **your** marriage, are you?* [you are/possessive]
>
> *Is **your** husband coming on the trip?* [possessive]

Exercise 3

Complete the following sentences with the correct words in parentheses.

1. I don't care _____ turn it really is.
   _____ going to do the cooking tonight?
   (who's/whose)

2. My friend's parents are still at _____ cabin in the
   mountains. It is snowing _____ at the moment.
   _____ planning to ski tomorrow morning.
   (they're/their/there)

3. _____ hard to get a good cup of coffee on this street.
   The only good coffee shop closed _____ doors about
   a month ago and moved to another neighborhood. (it's/its)

4. Where are _____ car keys? _____
   always losing them. (you're/your)

PART 4 ## VOCABULARY BUILDING

HOMOPHONES

Homophones are words that sound the same when spoken aloud, but that have
different spellings and meanings. They can also be different parts of speech.

*Just beyond the three kayaks crouched a damp **roll** of fog.* (lines 2–3)

Roll is a noun that refers to a round object.

*My favorite actor has the main **role** in the new Tarantino movie.*

Role is a noun that means *part*.

*"You're not trying," he said **through** clenched teeth."* (line 17)

Through is a preposition.

*Harry **threw** the ball at her with a great deal of force.*

Threw is the past tense of the verb *to throw*.

Exercise 1

Look at the following list of common homophones. Work with a partner to explain each pair. Try to do the exercise without the help of a dictionary or the Internet.

1. aloud/allowed
2. brake/break
3. cent/sent
4. flour/flower
5. lead/led
6. passed/past

7. rain/reign
8. sighs/size
9. stair/stare
10. waist/waste
11. wait/weight
12. weather/whether

DENOTATION AND CONNOTATION

Denotation refers to a word's dictionary definition. For example, the denotation of *fog* is "a thick cloud that forms close to the ground." **Connotation** refers to a word's associations. These may be positive or negative depending on the context. For example, the usual connotations of *fog* are negative. They include cold, danger, and difficulty seeing or thinking clearly. However, in a hot climate, fog could also have positive connotations such as relief from the heat.

Exercise 2

Make two columns called *positive connotation* and *negative connotation.* Look at the following verbs. Define each verb as it is used in the story; then place it in the appropriate column.

shivered (line 9)

drilled (line 21)

cajoled (line 21)

rewarded (line 21)

bullied (line 21)

shamed (line 21)

strained (line 25)

shimmered (line 29)

slammed (line 47)

hammered (line 48)

Exercise 3

What do you notice about your two columns? How does your observation relate to the story?

WRITING ACTIVITIES

1. Have you or has someone you know ever been the victim of a bully? Write two paragraphs describing what happened, how you (or the other person) felt, and whether anything was done to stop the bullying.

2. Describe an accident you have witnessed or were part of. Say who was involved, explain the cause of the accident, and indicate whether anyone was injured. Try to capture the emotions of the people involved.

3. Many films and television programs depict bad marriages. In the novel *Revolutionary Road* (1961) by Richard Yates, two people with very different personalities and dreams marry, with tragic results. A movie version starring Leonardo DiCaprio and Kate Winslet was made in 2008. Write a review of a book, movie, or television program that deals with a couple who shouldn't be together. Outline the plot, explain why the partners are bad for each other, and say what happens to them at the end.

6 Blackberries

Leslie Norris

(1921–2006)

Leslie Norris was born in Wales, but he lived most of his life in England and the United States. As a young man, Norris was influenced by the famous Welsh poet Dylan Thomas, and he knew from an early age that he too wanted to become a poet. He first worked as a teacher and then as a headmaster in England. Later, he was appointed Poetry and Creative Writing Professor at Brigham Young University in Utah. His collections of poetry include *Finding Gold* (1967), *Walking the White Fields* (1980), and *A Sea in the Desert* (1989). Norris also wrote several collections of short stories, including *Sliding* (1978) and *The Girl from Cardigan* (1988). In his lifetime, he won numerous awards for both his poetry and his short stories.

Blackberries

A small boy learns a difficult life lesson.

M r. Frensham opened his shop at eight-thirty, but it was past nine when the woman and child went in. The shop was empty and there were no footprints on the fresh sawdust shaken onto the floor. The child listened to the melancholy[1] sound
5 of the bell as the door closed behind him and he scuffed his feet[2] in the yellow sawdust. Underneath, the boards were brown and worn, and dark knots[3] stood up in them. He had never been in this shop before. He was going to have his hair cut for the first time in his life, except for the times when his mother had trimmed it gently behind
10 his neck.

Mr. Frensham was sitting in a large chair, reading a newspaper. He could make the chair turn around, and he spun twice about in it before he put down his paper, smiled, and said, "Good morning."

He was an old man, thin, with flat white hair. He wore a
15 white coat.

"One gentleman," he said, "to have his locks shorn."[4]

He put a board across the two arms of his chair, lifted the child, and sat him on it.

"How are you, my dear? And your father, is he well?" he said to
20 the child's mother.

He took a sheet from a cupboard on the wall and wrapped it about the child's neck, tucking it into his collar. The sheet covered the child completely and hung almost to the floor. Cautiously the boy moved his hidden feet. He could see the bumps they made in
25 the cloth. He moved his finger against the inner surface of the sheet and made a six with it, and then an eight. He liked those shapes.

"Snip,[5] snip," said Mr. Frensham, "and how much does the gentleman want off? All of it? All his lovely curls? I think not."

"Just an ordinary cut, please, Mr. Frensham," said the child's
30 mother, "not too much off. I, my husband and I, we thought it was time for him to look like a little boy. His hair grows so quickly."

Mr. Frensham's hands were very cold. His hard fingers turned the boy's head first to one side and then to the other and the boy could hear the long scissors snapping away[6] behind him, and above

---

1 **melancholy** sad
2 **scuffed his feet** scraped his feet along the floor
3 **knots** natural marks in wood

4 **have his locks shorn** have his hair cut
5 **snip** quick, small cut
6 **snapping away** cutting quickly with a clicking sound

35 his ears. He was quite frightened, but he liked watching the small tufts of his hair drop lightly on the sheet which covered him, and then roll an inch or two before they stopped. Some of the hair fell to the floor and by moving his hand surreptitiously[7] he could make nearly all of it fall down. The hair fell without a sound. Tilting his

40 head slightly, he could see the bunches on the floor, not belonging to him any more.

"Easy to see who this boy is," Mr. Frensham said to the child's mother. "I won't get redder hair in the shop today. Your father had hair like this when he was young, very much this color. I've cut your

45 father's hair for fifty years. He's keeping well, you say? There, I think that's enough. We don't want him to dislike coming to see me."

He took the sheet off the child and flourished[8] it hard before folding it and putting it on a shelf. He swept the back of the child's neck with a small brush. Nodding his own old head in admiration,

50 he looked at the child's hair for flaws[9] in the cutting.

"Very handsome," he said.

The child saw his face in a mirror. It looked pale and large, but also much the same as always. When he felt the back of his neck, the new short hairs stood up sharp against his hand.

55 "We're off to do some shopping," his mother said to Mr. Frensham as she handed him the money.

They were going to buy the boy a cap, a round cap with a little button on top and a peak over his eyes, like his cousin Harry's cap. The boy wanted the cap very much. He walked seriously beside his

60 mother and he was not impatient even when she met Mrs. Lewis and talked to her, and then took a long time at the fruiterer's buying apples and potatoes.

"This is the smallest size we have," the man in the clothes shop said. "It may be too large for him."

65 "He's just had his hair cut," said his mother. "That should make a difference."

The man put the cap on the boy's head and stood back to look. It was a beautiful cap. The badge in front was shaped like a shield and it was red and blue. It was not too big, although the man could put

70 two fingers under it, at the side of the boy's head.

"On the other hand, we don't want it too tight," the man said. "We want something he can grow into, something that will last him a long time."

---

7 **surreptitiously** secretly

8 **flourished** shook up and down

9 **flaws** mistakes

"Oh I hope so," his mother said. "It's expensive enough."

75 The boy carried the cap himself, in a brown paper bag that had "Price, Clothiers, High Street"[10] on it. He could read it all except "Clothiers" and his mother told him that. They put his cap, still in its bag, in a drawer when they got home.

His father came home late in the afternoon. The boy heard the
80 firm clap of the closing door and his father's long step down the hall. He leaned against his father's knee while the man ate his dinner. The meal had been keeping warm in the oven and the plate was very hot. A small steam was rising from the potatoes, and the gravy had dried to a thin crust[11] where it was shallow at the side of
85 the plate. The man lifted the dry gravy with his knife and fed it to his son, very carefully lifting it into the boy's mouth, as if he were feeding a small bird. The boy loved this. He loved the hot savor[12] of his father's dinner, the way his father cut away the small delicacies for him and fed them to him slowly. He leaned drowsily[13] against
90 his father's leg.

Afterwards he put on his cap and stood before his father, certain of the man's approval. The man put his hand on the boy's head and looked at him without smiling.

"On Sunday," he said, "we'll go for a walk. Just you and I. We'll
95 be men together."

Although it was late in September, the sun was warm and the paths dry. The man and his boy walked beside the disused canal[14] and powdery white dust covered their shoes. The boy thought of the days before he had been born, when the canal had been busy. He
100 thought of the long boats pulled by solid horses, gliding through the water. In his head he listened to the hushed, wet noises they would have made, the soft waves slapping the banks, and green tench[15] looking up as the barges[16] moved above them, their water suddenly darkened. His grandfather had told him about that. But now the
105 channel was filled with mud and tall reeds. Bullrush and watergrass grew in the damp passages. He borrowed his father's walking stick and knocked the heads off a company of seeding dandelions,[17]

---

10 **"Price, Clothiers, High Street"** name and address of the store
11 **the gravy had dried to a thin crust** the sauce had become hard
12 **savor** taste or smell
13 **drowsily** sleepily
14 **canal** artificial waterway for boats carrying goods
15 **tench** a type of fish
16 **barges** flat-bottomed boats used for carrying goods
17 **company of seeding dandelions** group of small flowers with fluffy white tops

watching the tiny parachutes[18] carry away their minute dark burdens.[19]

110   "There they go," he said to himself. "There they go, sailing away to China."

    "Come on," said his father, "or we'll never reach Fletcher's Woods."

    The boy hurried after his father. He had never been to Fletcher's Woods. Once his father had heard a nightingale there. It had been 115 in the summer, long ago, and his father had gone with his friends, to hear the singing bird. They had stood under a tree and listened. Then the moon went down and his father, stumbling[20] home, had fallen into a blackberry bush.

    "Will there be blackberries?" he asked.

120   "There should be," his father said. "I'll pick some for you."

    In Fletcher's Woods there was shade beneath the trees, and sunlight, thrown in yellow patches on to the grass, seemed to grow out of the ground rather than come from the sky. The boy stepped from sunlight to sunlight, in and out of shadow. His father showed 125 him a tangle of bramble,[21] hard with thorns, its leaves just beginning to color into autumn, its long runners[22] dry and brittle[23] on the grass. Clusters of purple fruit hung in the branches. His father reached up and chose a blackberry for him. Its skin was plump and shining, each of its purple globes held a point of reflected light.

130   "You can eat it," his father said.

    The boy put the blackberry in his mouth. He rolled it with his tongue, feeling its irregularity, and crushed it against the roof of his mouth. Released juice, sweet and warm as summer, ran down his throat, hard seeds cracked between his teeth. When he laughed his 135 father saw that his mouth was deeply stained. Together they picked and ate the dark berries, until their lips were purple and their hands marked and scratched.

    "We should take some for your mother," the man said.

    He reached with his stick and pulled down high canes[24] where 140 the choicest[25] berries grew, picking them to take home. They had nothing to carry them in, so the boy put his new cap on the grass and they filled its hollow with berries. He held the cap by its edges and they went home.

---

18 **parachutes** equipment used for jumping out of a plane (poetic comparison)
19 **minute dark burdens** poetic language describing the dandelion seeds
20 **stumbling** walking unsteadily

21 **tangle of bramble** a thick thorny bush
22 **runners** thin roots along the ground
23 **brittle** easily broken
24 **canes** stems
25 **choicest** best

"It was a stupid thing to do," his mother said, "utterly stupid. What
were you thinking of?"

The young man did not answer.

"If we had the money, it would be different," his mother said,
"Where do you think the money comes from?"

"I know where the money comes from," his father said. "I work
hard enough for it."

"His new cap," his mother said. "How am I to get him another?"

The cap lay on the table and by standing on tiptoe the boy could
see it. Inside it was wet with the sticky juice of blackberries. Small
pieces of blackberry skins were stuck to it. The stains were dark and
irregular.

"It will probably dry out all right," his father said.

His mother's face was red and distorted,[26] her voice shrill.[27]

"If you had anything like a job," she shouted, "and could buy
caps by the dozen, then—"

She stopped and shook her head. His father turned away, his
mouth hard.

"I do what I can," he said.

"That's not much!" his mother said. She was tight with scorn.[28]
"You don't do much!"

Appalled, the child watched the quarrel mount and spread.[29]
He began to cry quietly, to himself, knowing that it was a different
weeping to any he had experienced before, that he was crying for
a different pain. And the child began to understand that they were
different people; his father, his mother, himself, and that he must
learn sometimes to be alone.

---

26 **distorted** unnatural looking
27 **shrill** very high and unpleasant
28 **scorn** lack of respect

29 **Appalled, the child watched the quarrel
mount and spread.** Shocked and upset, the
child watched the argument get worse.

FIRST READING

A Thinking About the Story

Discuss the following question with a partner.

> What picture do we get of the boy's family and the place where they live?

B Understanding the Plot

Be prepared to answer the following questions with a partner or your class.

1. Why does the barber call the boy a "gentleman"? (line 16)
2. Whose father is Mr. Frensham referring to in lines 19–20?
3. Why did the boy's mother decide he needed a haircut?
4. The boy has several different feelings in the barber shop. Describe them.
5. How long has Mr. Frensham known the boy's grandfather? In what way does the boy resemble his grandfather?
6. How old do you think the boy is? Give reasons for your answer.
7. Why does the boy want a cap so much?
8. Why does the boy's mother buy a cap that is slightly too large for him?
9. How has the canal changed over the years? Give details.
10. What caused the boy's father to fall into the blackberry bush? (line 118)
11. Why is the boy's mother so angry after the boy and his father return from picking blackberries? Give as many reasons as possible.

PART 2

CRITICAL THINKING

A Exploring Themes

Reread "Blackberries." Then answer the following questions, which explore the story more deeply.

1. What do the haircut and the new cap represent in the story? In your answer, consider how the father reacts when he looks at his son in lines 91–95.
2. How do the personalities of the mother and father differ? Give at least three examples supporting your answer.
3. How does the boy change during the story? What does he understand at the end?
4. What does the incident with the blackberries show us about the relationship between the husband and wife?

B Analyzing Style

IMAGERY: ADJECTIVES, SIMILES, AND METAPHORS

Imagery is descriptive language that appeals to the five senses: sight, hearing, taste, touch, and smell. Writers use imagery to paint a detailed verbal picture, so that we can see and feel what it is like to be in a story.

Well-chosen **adjectives** can sharpen descriptions, making the characters, atmosphere, and setting more memorable. For example, as the boy walks along the *disused* canal with his father, his shoes become covered in *powdery white* dust (lines 97–98). With just a few adjectives, we get a sense of how the canal has changed from the busy waterway it used to be.

Similes are another type of imagery. A simile is a comparison that contains the word *like* or *as*. Similes that are creative and original can help us see something in a new or more intense way. For example, when the boy tastes the first blackberry, its juice is described as *sweet and warm as summer* (line 133).

Metaphors are comparisons that don't use *like* or *as*. Unlike in a simile, the comparison in a metaphor is implied rather than explicitly stated. For example, the flowers in lines 107–109 are referred to as a *company of seeding dandelions* with *tiny parachutes*. Through this metaphor, the flowers are compared to a group of soldiers jumping from an airplane. Because metaphors are not marked by *like* or *as*, they can be more difficult to see.

Exercise 1

Answer the following questions.

1. Look at the descriptions of the barber and his shop in lines 1–10 and lines 32–41. Which senses are appealed to in these descriptions? How do these descriptions help us understand the importance of the occasion and the child's feelings?

2. Look at the scene where the father comes home from work (lines 79–90). What simile is used to describe the father and son as they eat? What does this simile show us about the relationship between the boy and his father? What senses are appealed to in this scene?

3. On their walk to Fletcher's Woods (lines 96–109), the boy imagines the days when the canal was used for business. Choose several examples of the imagery in these lines and explain how they help contrast the present with the past.

4. Find the adjectives that describe the blackberries in lines 124–137. Which senses are involved in the description of the fruit? In what way is this scene similar to the scene where the father and son eat dinner?

Exercise 2

Complete the following sentences with an appropriate metaphor or simile of your own.

1. The blackberries were like _____.
   (simile)

2. The woods were as _____ as
   _____. (simile)

3. The mother's anger was _____.
   (metaphor)

4. The barber, a _____, frightened the
   boy. (metaphor)

5. Hearing the nightingale was like _____.
   (simile)

6. The dry canal was _____. (metaphor)

C Judging for Yourself

Express yourself as personally as you like in your answers to the following questions.

1. Do you think the father behaved irresponsibly?
2. Do you identify more with the husband or the wife? Explain your answer.
3. In your opinion, should the parents have waited to fight until the boy wasn't around to hear their argument?

D Making Connections

Answer the following questions in a small group.

1. In your culture, what significant event is connected to growing up: a religious ceremony, getting a driver's license, reaching legal drinking or voting age, or something else?
2. Is living close to nature desirable in your culture? Do children spend a lot of time outside?
3. In your country, what qualities are considered important in a good parent? Are they the same for men and women?
4. Who is usually responsible for family decisions relating to money in your country?

E Debate

Decide whether you are for or against the following statement. Write several arguments that support your view. Share your points with a classmate who has taken the opposite position.

   Childhood is the best time of one's life.

PART 3

GRAMMAR IN CONTEXT

WISHES

When we make a **wish**, we express a desire for something to happen that is unlikely or impossible. The correct verb tense or modal depends on whether the wish is for the future or the present.

- When we wish for something in the **future**, we use a **past modal**.

  *The boy wishes his parents **would** stop arguing over money.* [but they probably won't]

  *The wife wishes they **could** buy another new cap.* [but they probably can't]

- When we wish for something in the **present**, we use the **simple past tense**.

  *The husband doesn't earn enough money in his job. He wishes he **worked** somewhere else.* [but he doesn't]

  *The boy's mother wishes they **had** more money.* [but they don't]

- When expressing a wish in formal English, use *were* instead of *was* for the singular of the verb *to be*.

  *The boy wishes it **weren't** so dark in the woods.* [but it is]

  *I wish I **weren't** in the middle of my parents' argument.* [but I am]

  In informal spoken English you will often hear *was* instead of *were*.

  *The boy wishes it **wasn't** so dark in the woods.*

Exercise 1

Look at the following sentences. Complete each sentence with the correct form of the verb in parentheses.

1. He wishes his mother _____ him a cap.
   (can buy, would buy, bought)

2. They wish they _____ so much in front of their child. (do not argue, did not argue, will not argue)

3. The children wish their parents _____ them more. (love, loved, will love)

4. He wishes he _____ able to find a better job. (is, was, were)

5. I wish I _____ move to Argentina. (can, could, will)

6. She wishes she _____ her husband more. (can see, has seen, saw)

7. The boy wishes he _____ a way to help his parents. (can have, had, has)

8. My brother wishes he _____ more on his studies. (concentrates, could concentrate, will concentrate)

9. My young daughter often wishes she _____ an adult. (is, was, were)

10. Most parents wish they _____ their children from getting hurt in life. (can prevent, could prevent, prevented)

Exercise 2

Complete the following sentences in your own words, following the instructions in parentheses. The first one is done for you.

1. I wish I ____ate healthier food every day____. (wish about the present)

2. I wish I _____, but I have too much work today. (wish about the future)

3. The doctor wishes _____. (wish about the future)

4. He wishes he _____. (wish about the present with the verb *to be*)

5. My roommate wishes _____. (wish about the present)

6. You wish you _____. (wish about the future)

DIFFERENCE BETWEEN *WISH* AND *HOPE*

Wishes deal with unlikely or impossible situations. In contrast, **hopes** deal with situations that are more likely to become real. Hopes are more positive than wishes.

The boy wishes he could get a new cap soon. [it is unlikely]
The boy hopes he will get a new cap soon. [it may be possible]

The parents wish their lives would improve. [it is unlikely]
The parents hope their lives will improve. [it may be possible]

Hopes can also refer to the past if the outcome of a situation is still uncertain.

I hope I passed my exam. [but I haven't received my grade yet]

Exercise 3

With a partner, look at the following sentence pairs. Explain how the meaning differs in each pair.

1. **a.** He wishes his company paid him more money.
   b. He hopes his company will pay him more money.

2. **a.** They wish they could travel to Hawaii next month.
   b. They hope they can travel to Hawaii next month.

3. **a.** The writer wished he were William Shakespeare.
   b. The writer hoped to write like William Shakespeare.

4. **a.** My sister wishes she could go to Stanford University.
   b. My sister hopes she got into Stanford University.

PART 4

VOCABULARY BUILDING

STRATEGIES FOR GUESSING THE MEANING OF WORDS

A few basic **strategies** can help you work out the meaning of unfamiliar words without using a dictionary. This way you can read a story without stopping so often to look up words.

- Use the context to help you. For example, it is possible to work out the core meaning of *nightingale* (line 114) by noticing that the writer goes on to speak about a *singing bird*. Since the father and his friends went out at night just to hear it, we can also infer that the nightingale must have a particularly beautiful voice.

- Break compound nouns and adjectives into their separate parts. A compound noun such as *walking stick* (line 106) becomes clearer when we look at each word separately.

- Pay attention to prefixes and suffixes. For example, if you know that the prefix *dis–* indicates an opposite, you can easily figure out the meaning of *dislike* (line 46). Similarly, if you know that the suffix *–er* indicates an occupation, it may be possible to guess that a *fruiterer* (line 61) is someone who sells fruit.

  For more about suffixes, see pages 176–179.

- Look at the root of the word. For example, *minute* (line 108) is quite a difficult adjective. However, when you see that its base *min* is also in words like *minimum* and *minus*, you may be able to guess that *minute* means *small*.

Exercise

Work with a partner. Guess the meaning of the following words, using the strategies you have learned. Write your answers on the lines. Then, check your answers in a dictionary.

1. footprints (line 3) _____
2. worn (line 6) _____
3. trimmed (line 9) _____
4. cautiously (line 23) _____
5. admiration (line 49) _____
6. impatient (line 60) _____
7. disused (line 97) _____
8. clusters (line 127) _____
9. reflected (line 129) _____
10. irregularity (line 132) _____

11. crushed (line 132) _____

12. stained (line 135) _____

13. hollow (line 142) _____

14. tiptoe (line 152) _____

15. weeping (line 167) _____

PART 5 WRITING ACTIVITIES

1. When you were a child, was there ever something that you wanted badly? For example, maybe you wanted your parents to buy you a pet or a toy or to take you someplace special. Choose one memorable wish. Explain why it was so desirable to you. Say whether you eventually received it and whether it was as good as you expected. Try to use some *wish* and *hope* expressions in your writing.

2. Choose a place to sit and observe for at least a half-hour. It could be anywhere, such as a park, a café, or a bus. Use your senses to absorb what is happening around you. Then describe your experience using imagery that reflects these senses. You don't have to include all five senses, but try to include as many as possible.

3. "Blackberries" contains two important scenes that involve food. Both scenes show the loving relationship between father and son. Similarly, many films have used food to explore something deeper about life. The documentary *Jiro Dreams of Sushi* (2011) shows a Japanese chef who has dedicated his life to creating perfect sushi in a tiny underground restaurant. The movie *Julie and Julia* (2009) depicts the famous American chef Julia Child as she follows her dream to teach people the French way of cooking. Think of a movie you've seen where food has a central role. Briefly describe the plot and explain the role of food in the film. Say whether or not you liked the movie and why.

7 〜 Mr. Lupescu

Anthony Boucher
(1911–1968)

Anthony Boucher was born in California. He received a master's degree in Spanish and German from the University of California at Berkeley and could speak five foreign languages. Boucher started writing when he was young. His works include detective novels and stories that blend mystery, fantasy, and science fiction. In the 1940s, he also wrote many scripts for radio mysteries. His short story "The Quest for Saint Aquin" was named in 1970 as one of the best science fiction stories ever. Boucher was also an editor and critic, writing hundreds of reviews for the *New York Times Book Review, San Francisco Chronicle,* and other newspapers and journals. As a result, he is recognized as a central figure in the development of modern mystery and science fiction writing.

Mr. Lupescu

A young boy's imaginary friend causes trouble.

The teacups rattled, and flames flickered over the logs.

"Alan, I *do* wish you could do something about Bobby."

"Isn't that rather Robert's place?"[1]

"Oh you know *Robert*. He's so busy doing good in nice abstract ways with committees in them."

"And headlines."[2]

"He can't be bothered with things like Mr. Lupescu. After all, Bobby's only his son."

"And yours, Marjorie."

"And mine. But things like this take a *man*, Alan."

The room was warm and peaceful; Alan stretched his long legs by the fire and felt domestic.[3] Marjorie was soothing even when she fretted.[4] The firelight did things to her hair and the curve of her blouse.

A small whirlwind entered at high velocity[5] and stopped only when Marjorie said, "Bob-*by*! Say hello nicely to Uncle Alan."

Bobby said hello and stood tentatively[6] on one foot.

"Alan…" Marjorie prompted.

Alan sat up straight and tried to look paternal.[7] "Well, Bobby," he said. "And where are you off to in such a hurry?"

"See Mr. Lupescu 'f course. He usually comes afternoons."

"Your mother's been telling me about Mr. Lupescu. He must be quite a person."

"Oh gee[8] I'll say he is, Uncle Alan. He's got a great big red nose and red gloves and red eyes—not like when you've been crying but really red like yours're brown—and little red wings that twitch[9] only he can't fly with them cause they're ruddermentary[10] he says. And he talks like—oh gee I can't do it, but he's swell,[11] he is."

"Lupescu's a funny name for a fairy godfather,[12] isn't it, Bobby?"

---

1 **"Isn't that rather Robert's place?"** "Isn't that Robert's responsibility instead of mine?"
2 **headlines** newspaper articles that feature Robert's work
3 **domestic** comfortably at home
4 **Marjorie was soothing even when she fretted.** Marjorie had a calming effect even when she was anxious.
5 **velocity** speed
6 **tentatively** uncertainly
7 **paternal** fatherly

8 **Oh gee** exclamation of enthusiasm (old-fashioned)
9 **twitch** make quick movements that are not controlled
10 **ruddermentary** child's incorrect pronunciation of *rudimentary*; not fully developed
11 **he's swell** he's great (old-fashioned slang)
12 **fairy godfather** a fairytale character who uses magical powers to help a young hero or heroine

30   "Why? Mr. Lupescu always says why do all the fairies have to be Irish because it takes all kinds,[13] doesn't it?"

     "*Alan*!" Marjorie said. "I don't see that you're doing a *bit* of good. You talk to him seriously like that and you simply make him think it *is* serious. And you *do* know better, don't you, Bobby? You're
35 just joking with us."

     "Joking? About *Mr. Lupescu*?"

     "Marjorie, you don't—Listen, Bobby. Your mother didn't mean to insult you or Mr. Lupescu. She just doesn't believe in what she's never seen, and you can't blame her. Now, suppose you took
40 her and me out in the garden and we could all see Mr. Lupescu. Wouldn't that be fun?"

     "Uh-uh." Bobby shook his head gravely. "Not for Mr. Lupescu. He doesn't like people. Only little boys. And he says if I ever bring people to see him, then he'll let Gorgo get me. G'bye now." And the
45 whirlwind departed.

     Marjorie sighed. "At least thank heavens for Gorgo. I never can get a very clear picture out of Bobby, but he says Mr. Lupescu tells the most *terrible* things about him. And if there's any trouble about vegetables or brushing teeth, all I have to say is *Gorgo* and hey
50 presto!"[14]

     Alan rose. "I don't think you need worry, Marjorie. Mr. Lupescu seems to do more good than harm, and an active imagination is no curse to a child."

     "You haven't *lived* with Mr. Lupescu."

55   "To live in a house like this, I'd chance it,"[15] Alan laughed. "But please forgive me now—back to the cottage and the typewriter . . . Seriously, why don't you ask Robert to talk with him?"

     Marjorie spread her hands helplessly.

     "I know. I'm always the one to assume responsibilities. And yet
60 you married Robert."

     Marjorie laughed. "I don't know. Somehow there's something *about* Robert . . ." Her vague gesture happened to include the original Degas[16] over the fireplace, the sterling tea service, and even the liveried footman[17] who came in at that moment to clear away.[18]

---

13 **it takes all kinds** *It takes all kinds to make a world.* Variety is good, and differences should be accepted. (Saying)
14 **hey presto** suddenly, as if by magic
15 **I'd chance it** I'd risk it

16 **Degas** Edgar Degas (1834–1917), famous French painter
17 **liveried footman** household servant wearing a special uniform
18 **clear away** take away the dishes

65 Mr. Lupescu was pretty wonderful that afternoon, all right. He had a little kind of an itch like in his wings and they kept twitching all the time. Stardust, he said. It tickles. Got it up in the Milky Way.[19] Friend of mine has a wagon route up there.

Mr. Lupescu had lots of friends, and they all did something
70 you wouldn't ever think of, not in a squillion years.[20] That's why he didn't like people, because people don't do things you can tell stories about. They just work or keep house[21] or are mothers or something.

But one of Mr. Lupescu's friends, now, was captain of a ship,
75 only it went in time, and Mr. Lupescu took trips with him and came back and told you all about what was happening this very minute five hundred years ago. And another of the friends was a radio engineer, only he could tune in on all the kingdoms of faery[22] and Mr. Lupescu would squidgle up his red nose[23] and twist it like a dial
80 and make noises like all the kingdoms of faery coming in on the set. And then there was Gorgo, only he wasn't a friend—not exactly; not even to Mr. Lupescu.

They'd been playing for a couple of weeks—only it must've been really hours, cause Mamselle[24] hadn't yelled about supper yet, but
85 Mr. Lupescu says Time is funny—when Mr. Lupescu screwed up his red eyes and said, "Bobby, let's go in the house."

"But there's people in the house, and you don't—"

"I know I don't like people. That's why we're going in the house. Come on, Bobby, or I'll—"
90 So what could you do when you didn't even want to hear him say Gorgo's name?

He went into Father's study through the French window,[25] and it was a strict rule that nobody *ever* went into Father's study, but rules weren't for Mr. Lupescu.
95 Father was on the telephone telling somebody he'd try to be at a luncheon but there was a committee meeting that same morning but he'd see. While he was talking, Mr. Lupescu went over to a table and opened a drawer and took something out.

When Father hung up, he saw Bobby first and started to be very
100 mad. He said, "Young man, you've been trouble enough to your

---

19 **the Milky Way** band of light containing millions of stars in our galaxy
20 **a squillion years** an extremely large number of years (informal)
21 **keep house** manage a household
22 **tune in on all the kingdoms of faery** listen to the radio coming from a magical world
23 **squidgle up his red nose** make a funny expression (made-up word)
24 **cause Mamselle** because Mademoiselle (an unmarried French woman working in the house)
25 **French window** glass door that usually opens to the outside

Mother and me with all your stories about your red-winged Mr. Lupescu, and now if you're to start bursting in—"

You have to be polite and introduce people. "Father, this is Mr. Lupescu. And see, he does too have red wings."

105 Mr. Lupescu held out the gun he'd taken from the drawer and shot Father once right through the forehead. It made a little clean hole in front and a big messy hole in back. Father fell down and was dead.

"Now, Bobby," Mr. Lupescu said, "a lot of people are going to
110 come here and ask you a lot of questions. And if you don't tell the truth about exactly what happened, I'll send Gorgo to fetch you."

Then Mr. Lupescu was gone through the French window.

"It's a curious[26] case, Lieutenant," the medical examiner said. "It's fortunate I've dabbled a bit in psychiatry;[27] I can at least give
115 you a lead[28] until you get the experts in. The child's statement that his fairy godfather shot his father is obviously a simple flight mechanism[29], susceptible of two interpretations.[30] A, the father shot himself; the child was so horrified by the sight that he refused to accept it and invented this explanation. B, the child shot the
120 father, let us say by accident, and shifted the blame to his imaginary scapegoat.[31] B has, of course, its more sinister implications:[32] if the child had resented[33] his father and created an ideal substitute,[34] he might make the substitute destroy the reality . . . But there's the solution to your eyewitness testimony; which alternative is true,
125 Lieutenant, I leave up to your researchers into motive[35] and the evidence of ballistics[36] and fingerprints. The angle of the wound jibes with[37] either."

The man with the red nose and eyes and gloves and wings walked down the back lane to the cottage. As soon as he got inside, he took
130 off his coat and removed the wings and the mechanism of strings

---

26 **curious** unusual
27 **I've dabbled a bit in psychiatry** I know a little about psychiatry
28 **a lead** some helpful information, a clue
29 **flight mechanism** way of dealing with a difficult situation by avoiding reality
30 **susceptible of two interpretations** able to be explained in two ways
31 **scapegoat** someone who is made to take the blame for a bad situation or action
32 **has . . . more sinister implications** suggests a more troubling explanation
33 **had resented** had been angry at
34 **created an ideal substitute** made up a better alternative (to his father)
35 **researchers into motive** psychological experts who study the reasons behind a criminal act
36 **ballistics** the study of how bullets fly through the air
37 **jibes with** fits with, agrees with

and rubber that made them twitch. He laid them on top of the ready pile of kindling[38] and lit the fire. When it was well started, he added the gloves. Then he took off the nose, kneaded the putty[39] until the red of its outside vanished into the neutral brown of the mass, jammed[40] it into a crack in the wall, and smoothed it over. Then he took the red-irised contact lenses out of his brown eyes and went into the kitchen, found a hammer, pounded them to powder, and washed the powder down the sink.

Alan started to pour himself a drink and found, to his pleased surprise, that he didn't especially need one. But he did feel tired. He could lie down and recapitulate[41] it all, from the invention of Mr. Lupescu (and Gorgo and the man with the Milky Way route) to today's success and on into the future when Marjorie—pliant,[42] trusting Marjorie—would be more desirable than ever as Robert's widow and heir.[43] And Bobby would need a *man* to look after him.

Alan went into the bedroom. Several years passed by in the few seconds it took him to recognize what was waiting on the bed, but then, Time is funny.

Alan said nothing.

"Mr. Lupescu, I presume?" said Gorgo.[44]

---

38 **kindling** dry wood sticks
39 **kneaded the putty** squeezed the putty with his hands until it was soft
40 **jammed** pushed hard
41 **recapitulate** go over in his mind
42 **pliant** easily influenced
43 **heir** a person who receives money and property after someone dies
44 **"Mr. Lupescu, I presume?"** "You must be Mr. Lupescu."

PART 1 FIRST READING

A Thinking About the Story

Discuss the following question with a partner.

How many times were you surprised by the events in the story? Explain your answer.

B Understanding the Plot

Be prepared to answer the following questions with a partner or your class.

1. Why is Marjorie concerned about Bobby?
2. What does Marjorie want Alan to do? Why doesn't she ask her husband instead?
3. What is Alan's connection to Marjorie?
4. From Bobby's point of view, who is Mr. Lupescu?
5. Who is Gorgo? Why does Marjorie sometimes mention him to Bobby?
6. What kind of house do Robert and Marjorie live in? Give details.
7. What kind of house does Alan live in?
8. What sort of fantastic stories does Mr. Lupescu tell Bobby in lines 65–82?
9. What reason does Mr. Lupescu give Bobby for why he "doesn't like people"? (lines 70–72)
10. When Mr. Lupescu starts to threaten Bobby in line 89, what is he going to say?
11. According to the medical examiner, what are the two possible explanations for Robert's death? Rephrase them in your own words. Is either one correct?
12. Who is the "imaginary scapegoat" referred to in lines 120–121?
13. Who is the man in lines 128–138? What is he doing, and why?
14. What is Alan's vision of his future? (lines 143–145)
15. What happens to Alan at the end?

PART 2 CRITICAL THINKING

A Exploring Themes

Reread "Mr. Lupescu." Then answer the following questions, which explore the story more deeply.

1. Why was Robert killed? What evidence is there that the crime was planned very carefully?
2. How is Robert viewed by Marjorie, Alan, and Bobby? Give a separate answer for each character.
3. The name Gorgo suggests the Gorgon from Greek mythology. Look up *gorgon* in a dictionary or on the Internet. Briefly describe it and explain how it relates to the story.
4. There is a moral (a lesson) to this story. What is it?

B Analyzing Style

INFERENCE

There is a mystery at the heart of the story: who or what is Mr. Lupescu? The author doesn't want us to know the answer until the end. Therefore, he suggests many of the important points in the story instead of stating them directly. We have to **infer** these details by reading carefully between the lines. For example, Alan never directly says that he doesn't like Robert. However, he comments that Robert is interested in "headlines" (line 6). From this, we can infer Alan's opinion that Robert cares more about receiving praise than about helping people.

Exercise

Answer the following questions.

1. What can we infer from Marjorie's statement, "things like this take a *man*, Alan"? (line 10)
2. What is suggested about Alan's feelings for Marjorie from the way he looks at her in the firelight? (lines 13–14)?
3. Mr. Lupescu says he doesn't like people. What is the real reason that he doesn't want to meet Bobby's family? (lines 42–43 and 70–73)
4. What can we infer about Alan's profession?
5. What can we infer about Alan's economic circumstances? How is this important to the story?
6. What is suggested about why Marjorie married Robert? Explain your answer.
7. Why does Alan insist that Bobby tell the truth about what happened? (lines 109–111)
8. How does Alan feel after the murder? How do we know? (lines 139–140)

C Judging for Yourself

Express yourself as personally as you like in your answers to the following questions.

1. Why do you think Bobby wants to have Mr. Lupescu as a friend?
2. In your opinion, does Marjorie bear any blame for Robert's death?
3. How do you feel about the supernatural ending where Gorgo suddenly appears? Is there an interpretation that doesn't involve magic?
4. Do you feel that justice is served in the story?

D Making Connections

Answer the following questions in a small group.

1. How popular are fantasy and science fiction in your country? Name a well-known book, movie, or television show that features fantasy or science fiction. Explain its appeal.

2. Is the homicide (murder) rate in your country high? What are some of the more common reasons for killing?

3. Is it easy to own a gun in your country? Explain your answer.

4. What role do fathers typically play in the lives of young boys in your country? Are there stereotypes (widely held beliefs) about what a male role model should be like?

E Debate

Decide whether you are for or against the following statement. Write several arguments that support your view. Share your points with a classmate who has taken the opposite position.

The supernatural doesn't exist.

PART 3

GRAMMAR IN CONTEXT

MODALS AND MODAL-LIKE EXPRESSIONS

A **modal** is a special kind of auxiliary or helping verb that indicates the mood or tense of a verb. The modals are *can, could, may, might, shall, should, will, would,* and *must.* Modals cannot be pluralized; they do not change form; and they are always followed by the base form of the verb. The following examples illustrate some of the ways in which modals are used.

- *Can* and *could* express ability. *Can* shows that something is possible.

  Robert **can** *raise a lot of money for charity.*

  Could shows that although something is possible, it did not or probably will not happen.

  Robert **could** *raise a lot of money for charity, but he's too busy working.*

- *May* and *might* express that something is possible but not certain. In most cases, they are very similar in meaning.

  Robert **may/might** *raise a lot of money for charity this year.*

- *May* is used to ask for or give permission.

  *"**May** I leave the room?" Bobby asked.*

  Mr. Lupescu said to Bobby, "You **may** *go into your father's study now."*

- *Will/would* is used to express that something is/was likely to happen.

    *Mr. Lupescu thinks his plan **will** succeed.*

    *Mr. Lupescu thought his plan **would** succeed.*

- *Would* is used to express a repeated action or habit.

    *Mr. Lupescu **would** squidgle up his red nose and twist it like a dial.* (line 79)

- *Would* is used to express a wish.

    *"Bobby, I wish you **would** stop talking about Mr. Lupescu all the time," said Marjorie.*

- *Should* and *must* are used to indicate necessity. *Must* is stronger than *should*.

    *Marjorie thinks her husband **should/must** spend more time with Bobby.*

- To form the negative, add *not* after the modal.

    *Mr. Lupescu **cannot/could not** fly with his tiny red wings.*

    *Alan told Bobby that he **must not** lie to the police about what he saw.*

Modal-like expressions have the same function as modals, but, unlike single-word modals, some of them can change their form to agree with the subject. These expressions include *ought to, need to, have to, be going to,* and *would rather*.

- *Ought to, need to,* and *have to* are used to show necessity. *Ought to* expresses the weakest necessity, while *have to* expresses the strongest.

    *Robert **ought to/needs to/has to** pay more attention to his son.*

- *Is going to* means the same as *will* and indicates the future.

    *If you don't do what I want, I **am going to** call Gorgo.*

- *Would rather* indicates a preference for one thing over another.

    *Alan **would rather** be in Marjorie's house than his own.*

Exercise 1

Complete the following sentences with the correct modal in parentheses.

1. _____ you look so untidy just before your court appearance? (could, should, would)

2. Children _____ often play with imaginary friends without any harm. (can, must, ought to)

3. If you don't want to go to jail, you _____ obey the law. (can, may, must)

4. Every day Robert _____ shut himself in the library and make a lot of telephone calls. (ought to, will, would)

5. Marjorie wished she _____ turn the clock back to the day before the murder. (could, should, would)

6. This case is so unusual that we _____ require help from an expert. (may, ought to, should)

7. Bobby _____ make Gorgo disappear, in spite of trying very hard. (can, cannot, may)

8. Is Gorgo _____ return? (going to, need to, ought to)

9. Given more time, I _____ be able to solve the murder. (have to, might, must)

10. _____ I tell you a secret? (may, must, would)

Exercise 2

Complete the following sentences with a modal or modal-like expression. More than one answer may be possible. Compare your answers with a partner.

1. _____ you fire a gun with one hand tied behind your back?

2. Alan _____ live in a large house than a cottage.

3. The trial _____ take place next week.

4. The lawyers _____ call Bobby to testify. It hasn't been decided yet.

5. Alan _____ look at the Degas every time he entered the room.

6. You _____ not spoil a child. It isn't good for him.

7. Bobby wished that Gorgo _____ go away and never return.

8. Why _____ Bobby give evidence in the trial? He's only a child.

9. Alan _____ be punished. It is terrible to put the blame on an innocent child.

10. You _____ be right that Alan is the killer, but there is no proof.

Exercise 3

Look at the following sentence: *I will travel to a new country next year.* Rewrite this sentence five times, using a different modal or modal-like expression each time. With a partner, take turns explaining how each modal or expression changes the meaning of the sentence.

Exercise 4

Pick out five different modals or modal-like expressions from the story. Explain how each one affects the meaning of the verb.

SYNONYMS

Two words are **synonyms** if they have essentially the same meaning. For example, saying that Bobby's father was *mad* (lines 99–100) means the same as saying that he was *angry*. Learning synonyms will give you greater choice in your writing. They will allow you to vary your language so that you don't have to repeat the same words over and over.

Exercise 1

Look at the following sentences adapted from the story. Circle the adjective beneath each sentence that is closest in meaning to the word in bold.

1. The room was warm and **peaceful**. (line 11)
    a) calm   b) happy   c) unusual

2. When you talk to him like that, you simply make him think it is **serious**. (lines 33–34)
    a) anxious   b) important   c) sad

3. An **active** imagination is no curse to a child. (lines 52–53)
    a) fantastic   b) lively   c) physical

4. Her **vague** gesture happened to include the original Degas over the fireplace. (line 62)
    a) dull   b) unclear   c) unknown

5. Mr. Lupescu was pretty **wonderful** that afternoon. (line 65)
    a) interesting   b) marvelous   c) weird

6. "It's a **curious** case, Lieutenant," the medical examiner said. (line 113)
    a) common   b) known   c) odd

7. "It's **fortunate** I've dabbled a bit in psychiatry." (line 114)
    a) expensive   b) lucky   c) famous

8. The child's statement that his fairy godfather shot his father is obviously a **simple** flight mechanism. (lines 115–117)
    a) basic   b) distinct   c) unimportant

9. The child shifted the blame to his **imaginary** scapegoat. (lines 120–121)
    a) creative   b) incorrect   c) unreal

10. Time is **funny**. (line 148)
    a) humorous   b) peculiar   c) unnatural

Exercise 2

Match each word on the left to its synonym on the right. Its form may have been changed from the story.

_____ 1. abstract (line 4)   **a.** criticize

_____ 2. tentative (line 17)   **b.** disappear

_____ 3. blame (line 39)   **c.** genuine

_____ 4. depart (line 45)   **d.** intention

_____ 5. original (line 63)   **e.** leave

_____ 6. strict (line 93)   **f.** professional

_____ 7. expert (line 115)   **g.** rigid

_____ 8. horrified (line 118)   **h.** shocked

_____ 9. motive (line 125)   **i.** theoretical

_____ 10. vanish (line 134)   **j.** undecided

Exercise 3

Complete the following sentences with the correct word from the left-hand column in Exercise 2. The first one is done for you as an example.

1. Your idea for a movie is too _____*abstract*_____. Please give us more details about the plot.

2. The _____ for the murder is still unclear.

3. Only a(n) _____ is qualified enough to understand this problem.

4. Without strong action, rainforests will continue to _____ quickly.

5. Our flight to Istanbul is supposed to _____ at eleven o'clock tonight.

6. My grandmother is _____ by the amount of time I spend on the computer.

7. Our plans for the summer are still _____, but we'll know for sure next week.

8. My school is very _____ about not arriving late for class.

9. We couldn't believe it when we learned that our painting was a(n) _____ Picasso.

10. Don't _____ me for something that is your fault.

Exercise 4

With a partner, choose five synonym pairs from Exercise 2. For each pair, write a two-line dialogue using the original word in one line and its synonym in the next. For example:

A: Your plan is too abstract.

B: Yes, I know it's still quite theoretical, but I haven't had time to make it more concrete.

PART 5 # WRITING ACTIVITIES

1. When you were younger, did you have an imaginary friend? If so, write two paragraphs about the experience. In the first paragraph, describe your companion. In the second paragraph, say what effect the fantasy had on your life. If you never had an imaginary friend, offer an explanation for why not.

2. The ending of "Mr. Lupescu" leaves us wondering what will happen next. Imagine the next scene. Write a one-page dialogue between Alan and Gorgo, beginning with Gorgo's line, "Mr. Lupescu, I presume?" Your dialogue can be funny or serious. Try to include a variety of modals and modal-like expressions in your writing.

3. The fantasy genre is popular partly because it contains characters with magical powers. Books like *Harry Potter*, games like Dungeons & Dragons, TV shows like *Game of Thrones*, and comics like *X-Men* all feature people with superpowers. Pick one of your favorite characters with powers that you wish you had. First, give a brief description of the work. Then explain the character's magical powers, and say why they appeal to you.

8 ~ Niña

Margarita Mondrus Engle
(b. 1951)

Margarita Mondrus Engle was born in California. As a child, she heard her mother tell many stories about Cuba. She learned to appreciate her Cuban heritage, which features in much of her work. In addition to writing for both young and adult readers, Engle has worked as a journalist and a botanist. She was the first Hispanic writer to win the Newbery Honor for outstanding youth fiction, which she received for *The Surrender Tree* (2008). She has also written books in verse, including *The Poet Slave of Cuba: A Biography of Juan Francisco Manzano* and *The Wild Book* (2012), a novel for young readers. In addition, Engle has written two historical novels for adults, *Singing to Cuba* and *Skywriting*.

Niña

A visit to Cuba deeply affects a young American girl.

My mother was afraid it might be our last chance to visit her family in Cuba. The revolution[1] was almost two years old, and already there was talk of an impending[2] crisis.

At the airport in Miami she gave us three instructions.

5 "Never tell anyone you are tomboys."[3]

"Why?"

"They wouldn't understand. Also, don't tell the other children about your allowance.[4] You have more money in the bank than their fathers make in a year."

10 "So?"

"So, they would feel bad."

"Oh."

"And most important, don't bring animals into your grandmother's house."

15 "But Mom…"

"No animals. They don't like having animals in the house. Do you understand?"

At the airport in Havana we released the caterpillars[5] we had hidden in our luggage.

20 "Just in case there are no butterflies here," my sister and I reassured each other.

We had no idea what to expect, but the island did not disappoint us. Abuelita's[6] house was on the outer fringe of Havana,[7] and there were animals everywhere. We put lizards in beds, and tarantulas 25 and scorpions[8] in the living room. The fisherman who lived across the street gave us a ripe swordfish snout[9] to play with. When it really started to stink, my mother threw it on the roof, where it rotted quickly in the sun.

The fisherman's daughter asked me if I had money for ice cream. 30 "Yes," I said with pride, "I have eighty dollars in the bank, which I saved all by myself."

---

1 **the revolution** the Cuban Revolution (1953–1959), in which Fidel Castro established a communist government, resulting in a long conflict with the United States

2 **impending** coming soon (usually associated with something negative)

3 **tomboys** girls who act or dress like boys

4 **allowance** money regularly given to a child to spend as he or she wishes

5 **caterpillars** crawling insects that turn into butterflies

6 **Abuelita** Grandmother (Spanish)

7 **the outer fringe of Havana** far from the center of Havana, the capital of Cuba

8 **tarantulas and scorpions** eight-legged animals (arachnids) with painful, dangerous bites and stings

9 **snout** animal nose

"Dollars? Really?" I could see she didn't believe a word of it. I squirmed[10] inside, remembering my mother's admonition.[11]

"Well, I have something better," the girl offered. "Crabs. When my father gets home, you can have one to cook for your dinner."

She was right, of course. The crabs were better than my money. Her father came home with a truckload of them, bright orange crabs as big as cats. We put ours on a leash[12] and led it up and down the street until it died.

My sister liked dogs better than crabs. She begged my mother for a can of dog food for my great-grandmother's mangy hound.[13] We had to go all the way downtown, to Woolworth's, just to find dog food in cans. It cost more than a month's supply of real food, corn meal, black beans and rice.

Just to make sure there were no sins left uncommitted, I went across the street and told the fisherman's daughter I was a tomboy.

"Oh no," she said, horrified. "You're not a tomboy, don't worry. You will be fine." She fluffed her petticoats[14] and curled a lock of hair with her fingers.

My collection of revolutionary bullets was growing. They were everywhere—in Abuelita's front yard and in the weeds where we searched for tarantulas, which we caught with wads of gum attached to strings. There were bullets in the open fields beyond the city, and in the passion vines which clung to the walls of houses.

On one of my solitary expeditions I wandered far beyond those walls, beyond the open fields, and into a mud-floored hut with a thatched roof[15] and many inhabitants. The family greeted me as if I had some right to invade[16] their home. The children came outside to introduce me to their mule,[17] their chickens and the sensitive Mimosa plant which closed its leaves at the touch of a child's fingers.

One of the children was called Niña, meaning "girl." I assumed her parents had simply run out of names by the time they got around to her. In Niña's case, her name was no more unusual than her appearance. She was hardly there, just bones and eyes, and a few pale wisps of hair bleached by malnutrition.[18]

---

10 **squirmed** felt embarrassed
11 **admonition** warning
12 **leash** strap used to control an animal
13 **mangy hound** thin, dirty-looking dog
14 **fluffed her petticoats** tried to make her skirt look fuller (a feminine gesture)
15 **thatched roof** roof made of dried grass or leaves
16 **invade** enter without an invitation (usually refers to a military attack)
17 **mule** work animal that is a cross between a horse and a donkey
18 **bleached by malnutrition** colorless because of lack of food

"Doesn't she get enough to eat?" I asked my mother when I reached home.

"They say she has a hole in her stomach."

70　　One day I was standing in the sun of the front porch, watching a black storm cloud sweep across the sky, bringing toward me its thunder and lightning, which fell only in one small corner of the sky. A motionless circle of vultures[19] hung from the cloud, listless,[20] with black wings barely trembling in the wind.

75　　"Come in," my mother warned. "Don't forget your uncle who was killed by lightning, right in his own kitchen."

I ignored her. If it could happen in the kitchen, then why bother to go inside? I was just as safe outside.

Niña crept up to the porch, smiling her death's head smile, like
80　the skull and crossbones[21] on a bottle of medicine.

"Here," she said, offering me half of the *anon*[22] fruit she was eating. I took it. Together we ate and stared and smiled at each other, not knowing what to say. We both knew my half of the seedy, juicy fruit was going into my body, making flesh and fat, while hers
85　was going right out the gaping[23] invisible hole in her stomach.

Something like a shiver[24] passed through my shoulders.

"Someone stepped on your grave," Niña giggled.

"What do you mean?"

"They say when you shiver like that it's because someone
90　stepped on the spot where your grave will be."

I stared at Niña's huge eyes, wondering who could have been cruel enough to inform her that she would ever have a grave.

When we trooped[25] down the street to the bingo games at my great-grandmother's house, Niña tagged along.[26] An endless
95　array of uncles and cousins filed in and out, a few boasting[27] revolutionary beards and uniforms, but most outfitted in their farmers' Sunday best,[28] their hands brown and calloused.[29]

Niña was quiet. She poured burnt-milk candy through the hole in her stomach, and watched. The size of her eyes made her
100　watching feel like staring, but no one seemed to notice. Children like Niña surprised no one.

19　**vultures** birds that feed on dead flesh (vultures are often associated with death)
20　**listless** without energy
21　**skull and crossbones** symbol of death
22　***anon*** type of fruit (Spanish)
23　**gaping** wide
24　**shiver** shake from cold or fear
25　**trooped** walked together in a crowd

26　**tagged along** followed (often uninvited)
27　**boasting** displaying proudly
28　**outfitted in their farmers' Sunday best** wearing their best clothes, as if going to church
29　**calloused** skin thickened by hard work

On the anniversary of the revolution, the streets filled with truckloads of bearded men on their way to the mountains to celebrate. A man with a loudspeaker walked along our street
105 announcing the treachery of the Yanquis.[30] I was listening inside my grandmother's house. Suddenly his voice changed.

"Let me clarify,"[31] he was saying, "that it is not the common people of the United States who we oppose, but the government which has…" I stopped listening. Niña was at the open door,
110 smiling her bony smile.

"I told him," she said very quietly, "that you are from *Estados Unidos*.[32] I didn't want him to hurt your feelings."

At the beach, my sister and I went swimming inside shark fences.[33] We imagined the gliding fins beyond the fence. Afterwards,
115 our mother extracted the spines[34] of bristly sea urchins from the soles of our feet.

We visited huge caverns gleaming with stalactites.[35] How wonderfully the Cuban Indians must have lived, I thought, with no home but[36] a cave, nothing to eat but fruit and shellfish, nothing to
120 do but swim and sing. "We were born a thousand years too late," I told my sister.

With a square old-fashioned camera, I took pictures of pigs, dogs, turkeys, horses and mules. Not once did it occur to me to put a friend or relative into one of my photos. I was from Los Angeles.
125 There were more than enough people in my world, and far too few creatures. When my uncle cut sugarcane, it was the stiff, sweet cane itself which caught my eye, and the gnats[37] clinging to his eyes. His strong arms and wizened face[38] were just part of the landscape. When my cousins picked *mamonsillo* fruit, it was the tree I looked
130 at, and not the boys showing off[39] by climbing it. I thrived on[40] the wet smell of green land after a rain, and the treasures I found crawling in red mud or dangling from the leaves of weeds and vines. I trapped lizards, netted butterflies, and once, with the help of my sister, I snared[41] a vulture with an elaborate hand-rigged snare.
135 Our relatives were horrified. What could one do with a vulture? It was just the way I felt about everything which mattered to them.

---

30 **treachery of the Yanquis** the decision of the Americans to oppose Castro
31 **clarify** make clearer
32 *Estados Unidos* the United States (Spanish)
33 **shark fences** ocean barriers to protect swimmers from shark attacks
34 **extracted the spines** removed the needles
35 **stalactites** formations hanging from a cave roof
36 **but** except
37 **gnats** small flying insects
38 **wizened face** deeply lined face (from age or hard outdoor work)
39 **showing off** getting attention by proudly displaying their skill (negative meaning)
40 **thrived on** felt alive and excited from
41 **snared** trapped

If the goal of the revolution was to uproot happy people from their thatched havens, and deposit them in concrete high-rise apartment buildings, who needed it? Thatched huts, after all, were natural, wild, primitive. They were as good as camping. When my mother explained that the people living in the *bohíos*[42] were tired of it, I grew sulky.[43] Only an adult would be foolish enough to believe that any normal human being could prefer comfort to wildness, roses to weeds, radios to the chants of night-singing frogs.

I knew the hole in Niña's stomach was growing. She was disappearing, vanishing before my eyes. Her parents seemed resigned to her departure.[44] People spoke of her as if she had never really been there. Niña was not solid. She didn't really exist.

On the day of her death, it occurred to me to ask my mother, "Why didn't they just take her to a doctor?"

"They had no money."

I went out to the front porch, abandoning the tarantula I had been about to feed. As I gazed across the open fields toward Niña's *bohío*, the reality of her death permeated[45] the humid summer air. In my mind, I sifted through a stack[46] of foals and ducks, caterpillars and vultures. Somewhere in that stack, I realized, there should have been an image of Niña.

---

42 *bohíos* huts (Spanish)
43 **grew sulky** acted upset
44 **seemed resigned to her departure** seemed to accept that she would die

45 **permeated** spread throughout
46 **sifted through a stack** looked through a pile

PART 1 FIRST READING

A Thinking About the Story

Discuss the following question with a partner.

In what ways is the young narrator's trip to Cuba an exciting adventure for her?

B Understanding the Plot

Be prepared to answer the following questions with a partner or your class.

1. Why did the narrator's mother want to visit Cuba right away?

2. What three rules does the mother give her daughters before they arrive in Cuba? Do they obey these instructions?

3. Why doesn't the fisherman's daughter believe what the narrator says about her money in the bank?

4. Why doesn't the narrator's great-grandmother give canned food to her dog?

5. Is the fisherman's daughter a tomboy? (line 47) Explain your answer.

6. What signs of the revolution does the narrator see everywhere she goes?

7. What kind of home does Niña live in? Give details.

8. Why is Niña so thin?

9. What does the narrator mean when she says, "Children like Niña surprised no one"? (lines 100–101)

10. Why does the man with the loudspeaker suddenly change what he is saying about Americans?

11. What do you think the man said next about the U.S. government? Explain your answer. (lines 107–109)

12. What kind of work do the narrator's relatives do? Give evidence for your answer.

13. What do all the photographs the narrator took in Cuba have in common? (lines 122–130)

14. What happens to Niña?

15. What does the narrator regret at the end of the story?

PART 2 # CRITICAL THINKING

A Exploring Themes

Reread "Niña." Then answer the following questions, which explore the story more deeply.

1. How has the narrator changed by the end of her visit to Cuba?

2. In what ways is the narrator an invader when she visits Niña's home? (line 58)

3. Niña and the narrator seem to be about the same age, but their lives and personalities are very different. Compare and contrast the girls in as many ways as possible.

4. There are a number of direct and indirect references to death in the story. Find as many as you can and explain their significance to the story.

5. Explain the significance of Niña's name. (line 62)

B Analyzing Style

FIRST-PERSON POINT OF VIEW

We see the events of a story from a particular **point of view**. In "Niña" the narration is in the **first person**, meaning that the story is told using the pronoun *I*. Stories told in the first person only give us the perspective of the character who narrates the events. As a result, they are necessarily subjective rather than objective.

Since we see the story through the eyes of a young girl, we have to remember that she doesn't understand much of what she sees during her visit to Cuba. For example, when the narrator and her sister trap a vulture for fun (lines 133–134), she doesn't understand why her Cuban relatives react badly. From the point of view of her poor relatives, catching an animal that can't be sold or eaten is a waste of time.

Exercise

Answer the following questions.

1. Give several examples of how the narrator's youth influences her perspective on life in Cuba.
2. The narrator and her mother have very different perspectives on life in Cuba. Find at least two examples that show the contrast between their points of view.
3. Contrast the narrator's romantic fantasy of Cuban life with the reality of her relatives' existence.
4. When the narrator asks her mother why Niña wasn't taken to the doctor, what does the narrator reveal about herself? (lines 149–150)

C Judging for Yourself

Express yourself as personally as you like in your answers to the following questions.

1. How old do you think the narrator is? Explain your answer.
2. Why do you think the narrator's mother emigrated from Cuba to the United States?
3. What do you think the narrator's cousins in Cuba will tell their friends about their American relatives?
4. Do you think the narrator's trip to Cuba will affect how she thinks and acts in the future? Explain your answer.

D Making Connections

Answer the following questions in a small group.

1. Niña mentions the superstition (popular belief about luck) that when a person shivers, it means someone has stepped on his or her future grave. What superstitions do you have in your country?

2. There are many stereotypes (extreme generalizations) about American tourists. For example, many people think Americans don't know or care much about other cultures. How are American visitors viewed in your country? Do you agree with these stereotypes? How do you think people from your country are viewed when they travel abroad?

3. Has your country experienced a revolution in the last hundred years? If so, explain the circumstances.

4. In your country, is medical care easily available to everybody? Briefly describe the medical system in your country. Say whether you think it works well or whether it needs to be improved.

E Debate

Decide whether you are for or against the following statement. Write several arguments that support your view. Share your points with a classmate who has taken the opposite position.

Rural life is better than urban life.

PART 3 GRAMMAR IN CONTEXT

ADJECTIVE CLAUSES

An **adjective clause** is a dependent clause, meaning that it cannot be a sentence on its own. Like all clauses, an adjective clause must have a subject and a verb. Adjective clauses function as adjectives and modify (describe) a noun in another clause. They add details and give more information about nouns. Most adjective clauses are introduced by the relative pronouns *who, whom, whose, which,* or *that.* In the following examples, the adjective clause is in **bold** and the noun it modifies is underlined.

1. *Who, whom,* and *whose* refer to people. In informal English, you can sometimes use *that* instead of *who* or *whom.*

   • Use *who* when the pronoun is the subject of the adjective clause.

     *The fisherman **who lived across the street** gave us a ripe swordfish snout to play with.* (lines 25–26)

- Use *whom* when the pronoun is the object of the adjective clause. In spoken English, you frequently hear *who* instead of *whom*.

  The <u>fisherman</u> **whom we saw daily** gave us a ripe swordfish snout to play with.
- Use *whose* when the pronoun is possessive.

  The <u>family</u> **whose daughter was sick** couldn't afford a doctor.

2. *That* and *which* refer to animals, things, and ideas. They can act as the subject or object of an adjective clause. Sometimes you can use either *that* or *which*. However, do not use *that* directly after a comma.

   "I have <u>eighty dollars</u> in the bank, **which I saved all by myself.**" (lines 30–31)

   I looked up at the <u>vultures</u> **that were flying in the sky**.

3. When you use *that* or *whom* as an object, if it isn't separated from the word it modifies by a comma, you can omit the pronoun.

   At the airport in Havana we released the <u>caterpillars</u> **[that] we had hidden in our luggage**. (lines 18–19)

Exercise 1

Complete the following sentences with the correct relative pronoun. Use the rules that apply to formal English in your answers.

1. Their grandmother's house, _____ was on the outer edge of Havana, was an exciting place to explore.

2. I was introduced to the girl _____ had a hole in her stomach.

3. After I talked about the money _____ I had saved, I regretted it.

4. My relatives, _____ I had never met, were very kind to me.

5. My photographs failed to show the people _____ houses I had visited.

6. The crabs _____ we ate were the best I'd ever had.

7. My mother, _____ knew about Cuba, gave us instructions on how to behave.

8. Our mother removed the needles _____ were hurting our feet.

9. The children brought their dog, _____ approached us curiously.

10. The revolutionaries _____ we met treated us politely.

Exercise 2

Underline each adjective clause in the following sentences. Draw an arrow to the noun or pronoun it modifies. The first one is done for you as an example.

1. There was talk of an impending crisis that could threaten the two-year-old revolution. (adapted from lines 2–3)

2. . . . we searched for tarantulas, which we caught with wads of gum attached to strings. (lines 52–53)

3. The children came outside to introduce me to . . . the sensitive Mimosa plant which closed its leaves at the touch of a child's fingers. (lines 58–61)

4. The vulture, whose black wings were barely trembling in the wind, hung from the cloud. (adapted from lines 73–74)

5. "Don't forget your uncle who was killed by lightning, right in his own kitchen." (lines 75–76)

6. We visited huge caverns whose interiors were gleaming with stalactites. (adapted from line 117)

7. I thrived on the treasures I found crawling in red mud. (adapted from lines 130–133)

8. It was just the way I felt about everything which mattered to them. (lines 135–136)

9. I went out to the front porch, abandoning the tarantula I had been about to feed. (lines 152–153)

10. Somewhere in that stack, I realized, there should have been an image of Niña, whom I greatly missed. (adapted from lines 156–157)

Exercise 3

Which sentence in each of the following pairs is often considered incorrect in formal English? Rewrite it.

1. **a.** "The common people of the United States are not the people who we oppose." (adapted from lines 107–108)

   b. "The common people of the United States are not the people who oppose us."

2. **a.** I want to write letters to my relatives who live in Cuba.

   b. I want to write letters to my relatives who I met in Cuba.

Exercise 4

Complete the following sentences with an appropriate adjective clause.

1. Many people prefer living in a neighborhood _____

   _____ .

2. My parents, _____ , took years to feel comfortable in the United States.

3. Our cousin, _____, comes from Havana.

4. Summer fruit _____ tastes wonderful.

5. Families _____ often face many difficulties.

6. The noise _____ prevents me from sleeping.

7. Istanbul is a city _____.

8. I love the artist _____.

DESCRIPTIVE VERBS

Although Margarita Engle writes simple sentences, she uses many **descriptive verbs** in "Niña." These verbs not only push the action along, they also have an effect similar to adjectives, adding richness and color to her writing. For example, when Engle writes that the narrator _squirmed inside_ (line 33), the verb suggests two meanings at once. The first meaning is _nervously move from side to side_. The second meaning is _feel embarrassed_. Since we think about both meanings at the same time, the verb adds a descriptive layer to the writing, helping us understand how the girl feels inside.

Exercise 1

Use your dictionary or the footnotes to define each of the following verbs as it is used in the story.

1. reassure (line 21) _____

2. stink (line 27) _____

3. wander (line 55) _____

4. invade (line 58) _____

5. bother (line 77) _____

6. creep (line 79) _____

7. clarify (line 107) _____

8. extract (line 115) _____

9. vanish (line 146) _____

10. gaze (line 153) _____

Exercise 2

Match each verb from Exercise 1 with its appropriate context. The first one is done for you.

__4__   **a.** enter enemy territory

_____   **b.** have no particular direction in mind

_____   **c.** help someone understand a difficult concept

_____   **d.** walk late into a movie theater

_____   **e.** make someone feel better

_____   **f.** deal with a bee sting

_____   **g.** look into someone's eyes

_____   **h.** leave food in the garbage for too long

_____   **i.** leave home without telling anyone

_____   **j.** make an effort

Exercise 3

Complete the following sentences with the correct verb from Exercise 1. Use each verb only once.

1. Don't _____ taking off your shoes. We'll be leaving again in a few minutes.

2. Why does it _____ in here? You should open a window.

3. The dentist is going to _____ two of my teeth today.

4. A magician can make something _____ in front of your eyes.

5. I want to stay here and _____ at the ocean until the sun goes down.

6. When I visit a new city, I like to _____ around without using a map.

7. Philosophers argue about whether one country should ever _____ another one.

8. I don't understand your plan. Please _____ how it will work.

9. Many people are scared of animals that _____ along the ground.

10. My doctor called to _____ me that the problem isn't serious.

Find five more verbs in the story that help us picture what is happening. Use each verb in a sentence.

PART 5 # WRITING ACTIVITIES

1. Choose a place you have visited where the people were very different from you. Describe the main differences between you and the people there. Say whether you learned something about yourself from the visit.

2. Have you ever had a fantasy about living in a different place or time? Maybe you have imagined living in a different city or country, in nature, or even in a different century. Describe your fantasy and give the reasons for your choice. Try to use some adjective clauses in your writing.

3. Many books and films deal with culture shock, which is the feeling of confusion caused by being in a place where people are very different from you. Sometimes the contrast is presented with humor, and other times it is shown in a more serious light. In the movie *Lost in Translation*, two Americans in Japan become close to each other while experiencing culture shock. Pick a book you have read or a movie you have seen that deals with this subject. Describe the situation. Say whether you think the book or movie deals sensitively with the cultural differences.

CHOICES

Some Thing Blue
Transition
The Birthday Cake
The Kiss

9 ⇝ Some Thing Blue

Tayari Jones
(b. 1970)

Tayari Jones was born in Atlanta, Georgia. Her first three novels are set in the city of her birth. Jones earned a master's degree in English literature from the University of Iowa. She has taught creative writing at universities including George Washington and Rutgers. Her award-winning first novel, *Leaving Atlanta* (2002), explores what it was like to grow up during the Atlanta Child Murders (a two-year period when many African-American students were mysteriously killed). Jones's second novel, *The Untelling*, is the story of a family's struggles after a deadly car accident. Her third novel, *Silver Sparrow* (2011), is about a man with two families—one public and the other private.

Some Thing Blue

A young woman deals with the consequences of a promise she made.

In Scottsboro, Alabama, there is a warehouse store that sells everything that people leave behind on airplanes. This is where your mother has found your wedding dress.

You are apprehensive.[1] What ever happened to "something old, something new?"[2] What you have so far is something mortgaged[3]— this would be your childhood home. (Storybook weddings are far more costly than anyone imagined.) There is also something pawned[4]—your engagement ring, one and one third carats, clear as drinking water. (Your fiancé[5] Marcus, being both book-smart and streetwise,[6] haggled[7] with the pawn broker for almost an hour.) And now, there is this lovely gown—something ditched.[8] Because let's face it.[9] No one just loses a dress like this. (The designer is famous and photogenic; her picture is printed in gossip magazines.)

But how can you complain? Marcus is a good guy. He is a podiatrist.[10] More importantly, your mother is happy and she is *alive*. Only two years ago, she lay bald and dying, weeping because she would never be a grandmother, never wear the mother-of-the-bride dress she bought six years ago on sale at Filene's.

At the time, she really *was* dying, not yet in hospice care,[11] but fading, so you didn't tell her that lately you'd been dating women and that you loved one in particular, an artist who designed elaborate jewelry from bottle glass. Who would have benefited from such a confession?

Instead, you sat beside your dying mother and promised to name any son of yours Benjamin, for her father and you'd call any daughter Iris, in her memory. And while you were promising,

---

1 **apprehensive** anxious
2 **"something old, something new"** tradition that a bride should wear something old, something new, something borrowed, and something blue on her wedding day for good luck
3 **something mortgaged** a home used to borrow money from a bank (the home is lost if the money isn't repaid)
4 **something pawned** a valuable object exchanged for money (often in an emergency)
5 **fiancé** man you are engaged to marry

6 **book-smart and streetwise** well educated, but also knowledgeable about city life
7 **haggled** negotiated the price (negative connotation)
8 **ditched** deliberately left behind or thrown away (slang)
9 **let's face it** we can't ignore the unpleasant truth
10 **podiatrist** doctor who treats foot problems
11 **hospice care** program that gives special care to dying patients

you promised God you'd be a better daughter were you given just another chance.

And just like that, she recovered. So appealing was your offer
30 that God actually took you up on it.[12] Call it a miracle. Call it a contract.

So now you stand in the makeshift dressing room[13] of the warehouse-store laced into this gown[14] which was abandoned by a woman whose obligations[15] were far less urgent than your own.
35 The bodice is old-fashioned, rigid with whale bone but lush with beadwork.[16] The organza sleeves are light and thin as Bible paper.

Your mother waits on the other side of the curtain, eager and restless[17] as a child, her face shining with joy and with health. You love her. You love her. She is your mother. How dare you, even for
40 one moment, regret trading your own life for hers?

---

12 **took you up on it** accepted your offer
13 **makeshift dressing room** roughly constructed, temporary place to try on clothes
14 **laced into this gown** wearing a dress tightly closed with strings

15 **obligations** duties
16 **lush with beadwork** decorated with many small pieces of wood, glass, or plastic
17 **restless** impatient

FIRST READING

A Thinking About the Story

Discuss the following question with a partner.

Do you think the narrator made the right decision? Explain your answer.

B Understanding the Plot

Be prepared to answer the following questions with a partner or your class.

1. What does the warehouse store contain? What is its role in the story?
2. What is a storybook wedding? Why does the mother want one for her daughter?
3. How does owning a house help the mother pay for the wedding?
4. Where does the narrator's engagement ring come from?
5. Was the narrator's wedding dress originally expensive or cheap? How do we know?

6. What do we learn about the narrator's fiancé, Marcus? Give as many details as possible.

7. What happened to the mother two years ago? Why was she particularly upset?

8. Who is the jewelry designer? Why doesn't the narrator tell her mother about this person?

9. If the narrator has a son, what will his name be? Why?

10. What promise does the narrator make to God? Does she keep this promise?

11. When and where is the narrator telling the story?

12. What are the *obligations* that the narrator refers to in line 34?

13. How does the mother feel about her daughter's approaching marriage?

PART 2 CRITICAL THINKING

A Exploring Themes

Reread "Some Thing Blue." Then answer the following questions, which explore the story more deeply.

1. What kind of person is the mother? Give details that support your answer.

2. Why do you think the narrator chose Marcus for a husband?

3. What is the sacrifice the daughter is making for her mother? Why does she make this choice? Give as many reasons as you can.

4. The word *blue* in the title has two meanings. One reference is to a saying (see footnote 2). The other is to an emotion. Explain the two meanings.

5. The wedding dress, the engagement ring, and the money for the celebration are all presented negatively. List everything negative that we know about them. Pay attention to the words used to describe them, such as *mortgaged* (line 5), *haggled* (line 10), *ditched* (line 11), and *abandoned* (line 33). How do these words all relate to the narrator's mood?

B Analyzing Style

SECOND-PERSON NARRATION

Most stories are told in the first person (using the pronoun *I*) or the third person (using the pronouns *he*, *she*, and *they*). Unusually, "Some Thing Blue" uses **second-person narration**, which means that the narrator tells the story using the pronoun *you*. Since this form of narration is not often encountered in literature, the pronouns in the story stand out and immediately attract the reader's attention.

Exercise

Answer the following questions.

1. Who is the *you* in the story? Why does the narrator use this pronoun?

2. Throughout the story, the narrator addresses several questions to the person she calls *you*. Underline each one. Why do you think she asks them? What connects all the questions?

3. The story contains a number of sentences that begin with conjunctions such as *and, but, because,* and *so.* What is the effect of this style? How does it connect to the narrator's use of the second person?

4. There is a gap between what the narrator says and what she really feels. One place where we see this gap is in her description of the wedding dress (lines 32–36). On the surface, she is describing a desirable designer dress. However, her language makes the dress sound very uncomfortable. What words show how the dress feels on her? How does this reveal her true thoughts about the marriage?

C Judging for Yourself

Express yourself as personally as you like in your answers to the following questions.

1. Do you think any of the characters will be happy in the end? Consider the narrator, her mother, and Marcus.

2. What role do you think religion played in the narrator's decision?

3. The narrator seems sure that her mother would never accept the woman she loves. What do you think about this assumption?

4. How do you think the narrator will feel toward her mother and Marcus in the years after the wedding?

D Making Connections

Answer the following questions in a small group.

1. In your culture, do children respect their parents' wishes about whom to marry?

2. How do parents in your culture choose the name of a new baby? Are children usually named after somebody in particular? Do names have special meanings? If you were named after someone or something, explain the origin of your name.

3. What kind of wedding customs are common in your country? For example, you may discuss whether weddings take place over a few days, whether they are very expensive, what clothes are worn by the couple, and who pays for the wedding celebrations.

E Debate

Decide whether you are for or against the following statement. Write several arguments that support your view. Share your points with a classmate who has taken the opposite position.

Expensive weddings are a waste of money.

PREPOSITIONAL PHRASES

A **prepositional phrase** consists of a preposition followed by an object. The object can be a noun, or it can be anything that takes the place of a noun, such as a pronoun or a gerund. Examples of prepositional phrases include *at the time* (line 19), *with her*, and *after buying the dress*. Prepositional phrases function in similar ways to adjectives and adverbs. They add color and detail to sentences. The following examples show some of the ways in which prepositional phrases are used.

- When a prepositional phrase modifies a noun or pronoun, it acts similarly to an adjective. It gives more detail and helps answer the question *which one?*

    The narrator stands in the dressing room **of the warehouse store**.
    (adapted from lines 32–33)

    I tried on the old-fashioned dress **with beautiful beadwork**.

    The ring **on the table** *was shining brightly*.

- When a prepositional phrase modifies a verb, it acts similarly to an adverb. It tells us more about when, where, or how something happens.

    At the time, *she really was dying*. (adapted from line 19)

    You sat **beside your dying mother**. (adapted from line 24)

    Your mother's face shines **with joy** *and* **with health**. (adapted from line 38)

- Sometimes, a prepositional phrase can modify an entire clause.

    In my opinion, *we should have the wedding ceremony outside*.

- Prepositional phrases with *like* are used to make a comparison. They can be adjectival or adverbial.

    No one just loses a dress **like this**. (line 12) [adjectival]

    My mother cried **like a baby**. [adverbial]

Exercise 1

Look at the following sentences. Underline the prepositional phrases in each sentence. Indicate whether each prepositional phrase is functioning as an adjective or an adverb.

1. She moved like a ghost as she walked through the room.
2. Did you recognize the painting of my mother that's hanging above the door?
3. Please return the book with the green cover to the library.
4. In my opinion, the election will be very close.
5. I would love a strong cup of coffee from Kenya.
6. She saw the mayor of San Francisco on an airplane.
7. You should go to the doctor before traveling abroad.
8. A cat's eyes glow in the dark when you look at them.

Exercise 2

Complete each blank in the following paragraph with a prepositional phrase that fits the context. Share your answers with a partner.

When the bride woke up _____,
she felt _____. She rubbed her
eyes and jumped _____. She
searched _____ but couldn't find
her shoes. Her mother came _____ and
pointed _____. She knew her fiancé was
waiting _____. Her ring was lying
_____. She remembered how her fiancé
had negotiated _____. He had tried so
hard to buy the ring _____. She decided
that she didn't like the ring _____, so she
took it off, put it _____, and went
_____.

Exercise 3

Complete each of the following sentences with the correct preposition in parentheses. The prepositions are used as in the story. Check your answers by referring to the story.

1. My mother bought a dress _____ Filene's.
   (*at, in, through*)

   She loves to bargain _____ the salespeople.
   (*against, by, with*)

   She usually prefers items that are _____ sale.
   (*in, on, with*)

2. I recently read an unusual story _____ a gossip magazine. (*by, in, on*)

   A woman left her wedding dress _____ an airplane. (*at, inside, on*)

   It's strange how one person can benefit _____ another person's bad luck. (*from, out, to*)

3. I sat _____ my mother each afternoon when she was ill. (*against, beside, during*)

   I promised to name any daughter _____ mine Iris. (*for, like, of*)

   The room had a curtain, and I would wait _____ the other side when the doctor was there. (*at, on, over*)

4. When my mother heard I was getting married, her face shone _____ joy. (*by, out, with*)

   She was happy because she would soon be the mother _____ a bride. (*for, of, with*)

   She was completely unaware that I was trading my life _____ hers. (*for, through, to*)

5. When I got married, my heart felt _____ a heavy stone. (*about, like, near*)

   I missed the artist who made jewelry _____ recycled glass. (*from, like, out*)

   However, then I remembered my mother, and I got _____ my dress. (*for, inside, into*)

PART 4 **VOCABULARY BUILDING**

COMPOUND NOUNS

A **compound noun** is a noun formed by joining two or more words together. For example, a compound noun may be formed by combining a noun with another noun, as in *wedding dress* (line 3); a noun with an adjective, as in *grandmother* (line 17); or a noun with a prepositional phrase, as in *mother-in-law*. It is often possible to work out the meaning of a compound noun by looking at its individual parts.

Grammatically, a compound noun acts as a single unit. This means that it can be used as the subject or object of a verb, or anywhere else that a noun can appear.

Compound nouns can be formed in several different ways. Some are written as separate words, as in *wedding dress*; some are combined into a single word, as in *grandmother*; and some are hyphenated, as in *mother-in-law*.

Exercise 1

Look at the following compound nouns from the story. Make sure you know the meaning of each one. Complete the paragraph with the correct compound nouns from the list.

warehouse (line 1)	drinking water (line 9)
wedding dress (line 3)	gossip magazine (line 13)
engagement ring (line 8)	dressing room (line 32)

Two years after our wedding, I still look at my diamond
_____ every day. It's my most valuable
possession. I remember how long it took to prepare for the wedding.
My mother bought my _____ from a
_____ of lost items instead of from an
expensive store. I tried it on in a small _____.
Later I read in a _____ that it
was based on a gown worn by a famous actress. After the wedding,
we left immediately for a trip abroad. We were told to buy
_____ in bottles to avoid getting sick.

COMPOUND ADJECTIVES

A **compound adjective** is composed of two or more words that act together as a single adjective.

> Marcus was both **book-smart** and **streetwise**. (adapted from lines 9–10)

Usually, compound adjectives are joined by a hyphen when they are placed before the noun they modify, but they may lose their hyphen when placed after a linking verb.

> She is a **well-known** actress in our country.

> The actress is **well known** in our country.

Often the same word can be used to make many compound adjectives. For example, the adverb *well* can also be combined to form *well-built* (high quality) and *well-rounded* (good at lots of things).

Exercise 2

Look at the following compound adjectives. For each one, try to figure out the meaning from its individual parts. Complete the sentences that follow with the appropriate choice.

carry-on	part-time
good-looking	self-conscious
high-risk	sure-footed
old-fashioned	ten-page
open-minded	well-meaning

1. When she gives me dating advice, it's clear that my grandmother still has some _____ ideas about romance.

2. When people watch me running at the gym, I get very _____.

3. My _____ roommate gets all the attention when we go out together.

4. If you buy too many gifts at the airport, you won't be able to fit them in your _____ bag.

5. Don't hike up this mountain if you're not _____.

6. I need to get a _____ job to earn money while I'm at university.

7. I know my mother is _____, but I am old enough to make my own decisions.

8. Young people often engage in _____ behavior because they don't think about the consequences.

9. When I decided to become an artist, I was worried that my parents wouldn't approve, but they turned out to be surprisingly _____.

10. You need to submit a _____ proposal by next week.

Exercise 3

Each sentence below contains a compound noun or a compound adjective. Underline the compound noun or compound adjective. With a partner, discuss the meaning of each one.

1. My neighbor seems to have a great life, so I don't know why he's so mean-spirited.
2. Your mother's homemade jam is delicious.
3. When my father had a heart attack, I realized I should start eating healthier food.
4. I made a last-minute decision to fly home for my brother's graduation.
5. The real estate in this area is very desirable. You should buy your house now.
6. When driving, you should always use your turn signals to show which way you're going.
7. Your concern for our family is really heartwarming.
8. I like getting takeout food. It saves me a lot of time in the kitchen.
9. Checkout time at the hotel is 11 a.m.
10. Yosemite National Park in California is known for its high waterfalls.

Exercise 4

Do an Internet search for the compound nouns and compound adjectives in Exercise 2. For each compound noun or compound adjective, write a sentence that you find online that contains the word. Compare your results with a partner.

1. Most of us have made sacrifices in one form or another. Write two paragraphs on a sacrifice made by you or by someone you know. In your first paragraph, describe what was given up and the reasons for the decision. In your second paragraph, say what the effect of the sacrifice was on everyone involved and whether you think it was worthwhile.

2. Imagine what happens to the narrator and Marcus during the first year of their marriage. Write a monologue in which the narrator expresses how she feels on her first wedding anniversary. Topics you might discuss include the wedding, the honeymoon, and the couple's daily life. Try to use different kinds of prepositional phrases in your monologue.

3. Movies about wedding celebrations are popular around the world. Ang Lee's *The Wedding Banquet* (1993) features a young man from Taiwan who is getting married while keeping a secret from his parents. *Monsoon Wedding* (2001) shows a modern Indian family preparing for a wedding. *Rachel Getting Married* (2008) portrays an American wedding and the tension it causes between two very different sisters. Write a review of a movie you've seen that centers on a wedding. Summarize the plot and describe how the wedding is depicted. Make clear whether the movie is a comedy, a drama, or a mix of both. Say whether you recommend the movie.

10 ⌇ Transition

Patricia Grace
(b. 1937)

Patricia Grace was born in New Zealand. She belongs to New Zealand's Maori people, and her fiction centers on Maori culture, values, and concerns. Grace began writing while working as an elementary school teacher and raising seven children. Her first book, the short-story collection *Waiariki* (1975), won the PEN/Hubert Church award for Best First Book of Fiction. Her novel *Potiki* (1986) won the New Zealand Book Award for Fiction. Her other novels include *Dogside Story* (2001) and *Tu* (2004). In 2008 she was awarded the Neustadt International Prize for Literature. Grace has written four short-story collections and a number of children's books. She has also written a biography, *Ned and Katina* (2009), about a Maori soldier in World War II.

Transition[1]

A Maori family faces a life-changing decision.

The term Maori refers to the native people of New Zealand. Maori are believed to have arrived in New Zealand in the thirteenth century. Europeans arrived five hundred years later. They brought new diseases that caused great harm. Maori were also discriminated against and lost much of their land. In the second half of the twentieth century, Maori moved in large numbers to cities, where they faced severe problems. Many lost contact with their roots. Today there is increasing interest among Maori in preserving and practicing their culture.

See what they do, these grandsons and granddaughters of mine. Take these large stones from the river bed and put them here on the track[2] where each day I walk. This is what they do, these mokopuna,[3] and so to please them I walk with the bad leg that has
5 in it a feeling of deadness. This way and that, round and about the big river stones to make these young ones happy.

Home from school they will say to me, 'Did you walk today, Nanny?[4] Did you see our stones, our big river stones?'

'Yes,' I will say. 'Yes, I walked. This way and that. Round and
10 about the stones making the old leg all tired.'

'Ah Nanny. Soon we will have your leg all better. Soon. You'll see, Nanny.'

And then seeing how pleased they are, I will be happy to have done this for them. Not much time left now to give happiness to
15 these little ones. Soon this old light goes out.

And the mother too. This daughter of mine. Every morning this daughter gives me the work of kneading bread[5] in order to get the lame[6] hand strong once more. Sad this daughter. Sad to see this old one hobble about[7] with one side lame. And sad this old one to see
20 the daughter with yet another worry on her.

I tell her, never mind.[8] Never mind this old one. Look to the young. Look to the years ahead.

---

1 **transition** a change from one state or condition to another
2 **track** dirt path
3 **mokopuna** grandchildren (Maori term)
4 **Nanny** children's name for their grandmother
5 **kneading bread** squeezing dough by hand to make bread
6 **lame** weak, disabled
7 **hobble about** walk with difficulty
8 **never mind** don't worry about it

And yet this one asks herself what future there is for these dear ones of hers.

25   And a great sadness comes.

What future on this little corner of land, once enough to support many but now in these days merely a worry and a trouble. The ground dry and hard, and great round stones where once a river flowed. A great sadness comes, for this old one knows that soon

30 these ones must go away from this place. The city must claim these loved ones of hers, and in claiming take its price.[9] But nowhere for this old one in such a new place. Her place is here, and so the daughter has a sadness on her.

'Come,' she says. 'Come with your children. We cannot leave

35 you here. Before when you were well, though not even then happily. But now, since your illness?'

'Each day,' I say, 'I am a little stronger. Here I can walk along beside the river bed. Still I can take a hoe[10] in one good hand, still I can roll the dough for new bread, and have others here beside me.

40 My needs are few.'

But she is torn in two[11] this daughter.

I say to her, 'Here is the place where I was born and here is where I die.'

And the mokopuna who listen say, 'Don't talk so funny, Nanny.'

45 So I try to tell them there is nothing to fear.

'No need to fear a life ahead without an old nanny. This is just an old nanny with her light getting dim, who likes to see her days go by in this house, on this poor dried out piece of land where she was born.'

Then the husband, father of these little ones, stands firm[12] and

50 says, 'We cannot leave you here and if you'll not come then we stay too. This wife of mine and these children would fret away[13] in the town without their old lady.'

'Go,' I say. 'Here there is nothing.'

'And there?' he asks, and I know his meaning.

55 'The arrangements are made,' I say to him, 'and you must go.'

'Made before your illness,' he says, 'and now can be unmade.'

The mokopuna listen and are glad, and the daughter too.

'We can get along,'[14] she says. 'We have till now, and shall. This is a better place, a freer place, and our hearts are here.'

9	**take its price** require a sacrifice	13	**fret away** worry constantly
10	**hoe** farming tool for breaking up soil	14	**get along** manage, have enough food and money to live
11	**torn in two** pulled in opposite directions		
12	**stands firm** sticks with a decision (despite arguments against it)		

60   Look then at this daughter of mine, ageing before her time[15] with so much work, and this good son-in-law with the worry of bills to be paid and future needs to look to.[16] Then the children much too thin, and the older ones with little time for school work because of chores.[17] A great sadness.

65   Yet suddenly all these ones of mine are smiling, laughing because the good son-in-law has said arrangements can be unmade, and they will stay here with the old nanny on the dried-up place.

    'Ha Nanny,' they say. 'We will stay here with you now and make your leg better with our rocks. You'll see, Nanny.'

70   'And cook special food for you as the doctor said so you can live to a hundred.'

    All at once this old one is laughing too. 'Better for an old nanny like this to keep her old habits and go away happy, than live to a hundred on dried-up kai.'[18]

75   Away then happy to their jobs. Laughing, and happy to work till dark on this thirsting soil, and leaving this old one minding the days gone past.[19] Not long now, for the light grows dim. Not long now will this old woman hold these ones here, for soon this light goes out. These ones of hers will go from this place with some

80 sadness, remembering an old lady that once was their bond. But yet will depart with a new hope coming and a new life to make.

    This old one awaits that time, which is not long away. Not long. Then this old body goes to this old ground, and the two shall be one, with no more to be given by one or by the other to those

85 who weep.[20]

    And from the two—the land, the woman—these ones have sprung.[21] And by the land and by the woman held and strengthened. Now, from knowing this, the old one in turn draws strength as the old light dims, as the time of passing comes.

---

15 **before her time** too soon
16 **look to** think about
17 **chores** tasks that are done regularly at home
18 **kai** food (Maori term)

19 **minding the days gone past** thinking a lot about the past
20 **weep** cry because of strong emotion
21 **have sprung** have come into existence, have been born

A Thinking About the Story

Discuss the following question with a partner.

What attitude toward old age is represented in this story? Explain your answer.

B Understanding the Plot

Be prepared to answer the following questions with a partner or your class.

1. Why do the grandchildren place big stones in their grandmother's path?
2. What does the grandmother mean when she says, "Soon this old light goes out"? (line 15)
3. What does the daughter do to help keep the grandmother active?
4. Why does the family need to leave their land?
5. Did the family ever plan to move without the grandmother? Explain your answer.
6. What does the grandmother tell the family to do?
7. Why does the grandmother insist on staying?
8. What reason does the son-in-law give for changing his mind about going to the city?
9. What worries do the daughter and the son-in-law have?
10. What does the grandmother mean when she says, "Better for an old nanny like this to keep her old habits and go away happy, than live to a hundred on dried-up kai"? (lines 72–74)
11. What does the grandmother think her family will do after she dies?
12. Who or what do *one* and *the other* refer to in line 84? Why does the narrator compare them? Who are *these ones* in line 86?

PART 2

CRITICAL THINKING

A Exploring Themes

Reread "Transition." Then answer the following questions, which explore the story more deeply.

1. When we talk about a person's *roots*, we are referring to the place or culture of his or her ancestors. Discuss the importance of roots in "Transition."
2. What does the city represent? Consider both its positive and its negative aspects. What "price" does it take from the people who move there? (lines 30–31)
3. What attitude toward family is portrayed in the story?
4. Discuss the significance of the title. What transitions are examined in the story?

B Analyzing Style

NARRATIVE VOICE

The **voice** of a narrator is the distinctive pattern of thought and speech that makes him or her unique. Voice can include unusual grammar and vocabulary, as well as the particular way that the narrator views the world.

In "Transition," the voice of the grandmother stands out. Her first-person narrative is told in straightforward sentences as well as sentence fragments. She uses simple vocabulary and often repeats the same phrases. Her language has the rhythm of spoken rather than written English. She seems to be addressing the reader directly. Her voice makes the narrator sound like someone telling a story for future generations. She speaks in a voice filled with the wisdom of age.

Exercise

Answer the following questions.

1. How does the narrator's language, such as her choice of words and her nonstandard sentence structure, reflect who she is? Use quotes from the story to explain your answer.
2. Give some examples of repetition in the story. What is the effect of this repetition?
3. What are the dominant verb tenses in the story? What is the effect of using these tenses?
4. How does the narrative voice change starting at line 75? What is the main point that is made in the final three paragraphs?

C Judging for Yourself

Express yourself as personally as you like in your answers to the following questions.

1. Do you think the grandmother was selfish to insist on staying? Why or why not?

2. In your opinion, does the husband make the right decision? Explain your answer.

3. Do you agree with the daughter's statement that their home in the country is a "better place, a freer place" than the town? (lines 58–59) Explain your answer.

D Making Connections

Answer the following questions in a small group.

1. What position do old people occupy in your culture? Are they respected? Do they live with their families? What problems do they face?

2. What is life like for people who live in rural areas in your country?

3. Do many people move from one part of your country to another? If so, give the reasons. If not, say why not.

4. Are there groups of people in your country who are concerned about losing their traditional culture? Say who they are and explain why their culture is at risk.

E Debate

Decide whether you are for or against the following statement. Write several arguments that support your view. Share your points with a classmate who has taken the opposite position.

Quality of life is more important than living as long as possible.

THE SIMPLE PRESENT AND THE PRESENT PROGRESSIVE

Many students confuse the **simple present** and the **present progressive**. The choice of one or the other depends on the meaning you want to express.

The **simple present** is used in the following ways:

- To express a habitual or repeated action

    *Every morning this daughter **gives** me the work of kneading bread.* (lines 16–17)

- To express a fact

    *Everybody **dies**.*

    *The sun **rises** in the east.*

- To indicate that something is scheduled to happen in the future

    *The ceremony **starts** at nine o'clock tonight.*

- To tell a story in the present

    *The mokopuna **listen** and **are** glad.* (line 57)

The **present progressive** is used in the following ways:

- To show that an action is taking place at a particular moment and hasn't yet finished

    *Yet suddenly all these ones of mine **are smiling** . . . because the good son-in-law has said arrangements can be unmade.* (lines 65–66)

- To express that an action is going to happen in the future

    *My family **is moving** to the city next month.*

- To express an action that is for a limited period of time only

    *My brother **is working** on a farm this summer.*

- To express an action that is happening around the time of speaking, but not necessarily at that exact moment

    *We **are planning** a trip to New Zealand in the summer.*

Exercise 1

Complete the following sentences with the simple present or the present progressive of the verb in parentheses. Compare your answers with a partner.

1. The husband and wife _____ a move to the city. (consider)

2. The grandmother _____ every day about her family's problems. (worry)

3. The children aren't here. They _____ stones on the path to help their grandmother strengthen her leg. (place)

4. We _____ the next three months planting crops. (spend)

5. It _____ for the first time in months, so the family is very happy. (rain)

6. Our train for the city _____ Tuesday at 11 A.M. (leave)

7. When Maori children _____ to the city, they have a hard time fitting in at school. (move)

8. I _____ a book about the Maori people. (write)

9. My students always _____ me with my research. (help)

10. Every semester I _____ a course on the history of New Zealand. (teach)

Exercise 2

With a partner, take turns explaining the difference between the following pairs of sentences.

1. **a.** I travel to Asia for my job.
   b. I am traveling to Asia for my job.

2. **a.** All of our children play football.
   b. All of our children are playing football.

3. **a.** Cats hunt silently.
   b. The cats are hunting silently.

4. **a.** What do you read for pleasure?
   b. What are you reading for pleasure?

5. **a.** The plane lands at 4 o'clock.
   b. The plane is landing.

6. **a.** The sun sets in the west.
   b. The sun is setting in the west.

7. **a.** My daughter is studying at Harvard.
   b. My daughter is studying in the library at Harvard.

8. **a.** I receive a lot of awards for my research.
   b. I receive an award for my research tomorrow.

STATIVE VERBS

Most verbs are **action** verbs. Action verbs can take the present-progressive tense. However, some verbs—called **stative** verbs—do not normally take the present progressive tense. Stative verbs usually express a state or situation rather than an action. They include *believe, belong, cost, hate, know, like, love, mean, need, own, prefer, remember,* and *understand.*

> *This farm belongs to my family.* [Correct]
>
> *This farm is belonging to my family.* [Incorrect]

Some verbs, such as *think, have,* and *see,* can have either a stative meaning or an action meaning depending on their context.

Stative: *I **think** it would be a mistake to move to the city.* [meaning *believe*]

Action: *I **am thinking of** moving to the city.* [meaning *considering*]

Stative: *We **have** an idea for helping our grandmother.* [meaning *possess*]

Action: *We **are having** a hard time in the city.* [meaning *experiencing*]

Stative: *Do you **see** what I mean?* [meaning *understand*]

Action: ***Are** you **seeing** your girlfriend this weekend?* [meaning *meeting*]

Exercise 3

In each of the following sentences, decide whether the verb has a stative or an action meaning. If the verb form is incorrect, write the sentence correctly.

1. The red car outside is belonging to my friend.
2. I am preferring the city to the country.
3. The boy remembers when he crashed his bicycle and broke his leg.
4. The chef is cooking for sixty people tonight.
5. My sister is knowing how to make a fire in the woods.
6. This plane ticket costs too much.
7. Are you needing help with your homework?
8. My parents drive twenty miles to work each morning.
9. I am loving you.
10. The children don't see why they have to practice the piano every day.

PART 4

VOCABULARY BUILDING

EUPHEMISM

A **euphemism** is an expression that refers to something uncomfortable in a softer, more acceptable way. For example, when the grandmother talks about dying, she says she wants to *go away happy* (lines 72–74). Here, she uses *go away* instead of the more direct word *die*. Death is a subject that has inspired many euphemisms. These include *pass away, cross over to the other side*, and *meet one's maker*.

Exercise 1

With a partner, look at the following euphemisms. With the help of a dictionary or the Internet, write the meaning of each euphemism in the blank provided.

1. between jobs _____
2. the birds and the bees _____
3. well-off _____
4. casualty _____
5. correctional facility _____

6. low-income _____
7. expecting _____
8. plus-size _____
9. pre-owned _____
10. restroom _____

Exercise 2

Complete the following sentences with the appropriate euphemism from the list in Exercise 1.

1. Governments usually don't like to speak about the _____ rate in a war.

2. Parents often have trouble deciding when to talk to their children about _____.

3. I was told that all the _____ cars had been carefully inspected.

4. Although she is the most _____ person I know, my neighbor drives an old, inexpensive car.

5. Fashion designers have been criticized for ignoring the needs of _____ people.

6. "Congratulations! I just heard that your wife is _____."

7. I hated telling my parents that I was _____ and therefore needed a loan.

8. My city is starting a program to increase the number of
_____ young people who go to college.

9. The more coffee you drink, the more you need to use the

_____ .

10. I hear that one of my classmates stole a car and spent a year in a

_____ .

COLLOCATIONS WITH *MAKE* AND *DO*

A **collocation** is a group of words that often occur together. Learning how to use the right collocations will help you make fewer statements that sound wrong to a native speaker. For example, we say *heavy traffic* (not *strong traffic*), *business trip* (not *business journey*), and *lions roar* (not *lions howl*).

There are several common collocations with the verb *make* in "Transition," such as *make arrangements* (line 55) and *make a new life* (lines 80–81). It is easy to confuse when to use *make* and when to use *do*. For example, one never *makes business* but *does business*, and one never *does plans* but *makes plans*.

Exercise 3

With a partner, complete the following paragraph by using *make* or *do* to form the correct collocations. Check your answers in a dictionary or with your teacher.

When they move to the city, Maori children _____
an effort to catch up with the other students in their class, trying
hard not to _____ too many mistakes. They
_____ their best each day. After school, they
have to help their mother _____ dinner and
then afterwards they have to _____ the dishes.
"_____ me a favor and don't _____
a mess in the kitchen," their mother pleads. After they have finished their
chores, they _____ their homework. They know that
their father works hard to _____ enough money to
support his family. The first few months are very difficult for the family
as they try to _____ a plan for their new life in the city.
The family knows that nobody will _____ an exception
for them. They have to _____ their very best all the time
and they _____ the decision never to complain about
their difficult situation.

Exercise 4

Write five new sentences using collocations with *make* and *do* from Exercise 3.

PART 5

WRITING ACTIVITIES

1. Have you ever had to leave your home and move to a new place? Perhaps you left to study or work, or your family moved to another country. Write a few paragraphs in which you express your feelings about this move. Try to consider both positive and negative aspects of the experience. If you have never moved, imagine how you would feel if you needed to do so; write at least two paragraphs explaining your feelings.

2. Consider how you feel about aging. Make two columns. In the first column list the advantages of old age as you see them. In the second column list the disadvantages. Then write a paragraph saying whether you look forward to growing old or fear it. Give reasons for your answer.

3. The New Zealand movie *Whale Rider* (2002) is a drama involving a Maori family. A young girl's grandfather is the leader of his tribe, and she is his closest living relative. However, he refuses to allow her to become the next chief because she is female. The film shows the granddaughter's determination, despite many obstacles, to become the leader of her tribe. Choose a movie you've seen that centers on a native ethnic group. Write a review outlining the plot. Say what you learned about the way of life of the people in the film. Share your review with your classmates.

11 ⇛ The Birthday Cake

Daniel Lyons

(b. 1960)

Daniel Lyons was born in Massachusetts. He received a master of fine arts from the University of Michigan. Lyons has held senior editorial positions at *Forbes* and *Newsweek,* as well as at the popular technology blog *ReadWrite.* In 2006 he created *The Secret Diary of Steve Jobs,* a blog based on the Apple co-founder. It quickly became popular and entertained over a million visitors with its insights and humor. Lyons's fiction includes the short-story collection *The Last Good Man* (1993) and the novel *Dog Days* (1998). He also wrote *Options* (2007), a humorous fictional biography of Steve Jobs. Lyons was awarded a National Endowment for the Arts Literary Fellowship. He was named one of the "Fabulous 52" in the 1996 Best Young American Novelists competition sponsored by *Granta* magazine.

The Birthday Cake

A child's birthday leads to a bitter conflict between two women.

The air was cold and the daylight was draining[1] from the sky. The street smelled of rotten fruit left in the carts and although this was a sour smell it was not altogether unpleasant. Lucia was accustomed to[2] this odor, and because it reminded her of the
5 feast days when she was a girl she enjoyed it, the way she imagined people on farms enjoyed the smell of manure.[3]

It was past six and the shops on Newbury Street were closed, but she knew that Lorenzo would stay open for her. She did not hurry: she was an old woman, and age had spoiled her legs. They
10 were thick now, and water heavy, and when she walked her hips grew sore from the effort of moving them.

She stopped by a bench, wanting to sit but knowing that to stoop and then to rise would be more difficult than simply to lean against the backrest. She waited for her breathing to slow, then
15 walked the last block to the bakery. Lorenzo would be there. He would wait. Hadn't she come to the bakery every Saturday since the war?[4] And hadn't she bought the same white cake with chocolate frosting, Nico's favorite?

"Buona sera, Signora Ronsavelli,"[5] he said as the chime[6]
20 clanged and the heavy glass door closed behind her. "You had me concerned."[7]

Lorenzo Napoli was too young to be so worried all the time. She wondered about him. She did not trust him the way she had trusted his father.
25 Standing before the pastry case was Maria Mendez, the little Puerto Rican girl who worked at the laundry. "Este es la señora,"[8] Lorenzo said to her. They were everywhere now, these Puerto Ricans, all over the neighborhood with their loud cars and shouting children and men drinking beer on the sidewalk. Now the rents
30 were increasing and the real estate people wanted the Italians to move to nursing homes. Even Father D'Agostino was helping them. "Lucia," the priest had told her, "you'd have company there."

---

1 **draining** disappearing slowly (figurative language)
2 **accustomed to** used to
3 **manure** animal waste added to soil to help grow food
4 **the war** World War II

5 **"Buona sera, Signora Ronsavelli"** "Good evening, Mrs. Ronsavelli" (Italian)
6 **chime** bell sound when a door opens
7 **"You had me concerned."** "I was worried about you."
8 **"Este es la señora"** "This is the lady" (Spanish)

This Maria from the laundry had a child but no husband. She smiled at Lucia, then peered down into the glass case.

"Miss Mendez needs to ask you a favor," the baker said.

Lucia removed her leather gloves and put them into her purse. "A favor?"

"My little girl," Maria said. "Today is her birthday. She's seven years old today."

"You must know little Teresa," Lorenzo said.

"Yes," Lucia said. She had indeed seen the child, out with her friends tearing up the vegetable gardens in the backyards.

"And I was so busy today at the laundry, so busy, all day long there was a line, and I couldn't get out to buy her a birthday cake."

"Yes." Lucia remembered that it had taken her two days to fix the stakes[9] for her tomato plants.

"Let me explain," Lorenzo said. "Miss Mendez needs a cake, and I have none left, except yours. I told her that you were my best customer, and of course we'd have to wait and ask you."

"All the other bakeries are closed," Maria said. "It's my little girl's birthday."

Lucia's hands began to shake. She remembered what the doctor had said about getting angry; but this was too much. "Every week I buy my cake. For how many years? And now this *muli*[10] comes in and you just give it away?"

"Lucy." Lorenzo held out his hands like a little boy. "Don't get angry. Please, Lucy."

"No. Not Lucy." She tapped her chest with her finger. "Lucia."

"Lucy, please," he said.

"No 'Please, Lucy.' No parlare Inglese. Italiano."[11]

"I could give you some sugar cookies," he said. "Or some cannolis.[12] I just made them. They're beautiful."

"Once a week I come here and I buy Nico's cake."

Lorenzo tipped his head to the side. He seemed to be about to say something, but then he stopped. He waited another moment.

"Lucia, think of the poor little girl," he said. "It's her birthday."

"Then bake her a cake. You do the favor, if you like her so much."

"Lucia, there's no time." The party was going to begin in a few minutes, he said. Besides, he had already cleaned his equipment and put away his flour and eggs and sugar.

---

9 **stakes** sticks that support a growing plant
10 *muli* a racist insult (Italian)
11 **"No parlare Inglese. Italiano."** "Don't speak English. Speak Italian."
12 **cannolis** Italian desserts filled with cream

"Lucia," he said, "it's the right thing. Ask yourself, what would Nico do? Or my father?"

"I know what they wouldn't do. They wouldn't forget who their people were. They wouldn't start speaking Spanish for the *mulis*."

75 She stared at him until he looked away. Outside, the wind had lifted a newspaper from the sidewalk and was pressing the leaves against the front window of the bakery. From somewhere on Common Street came the sound of a car's engine racing. She thought of Nico, how when he lay sick in bed during his last days 80 she had gone outside and asked the children not to make noise and they'd laughed and told her to go back inside, crazy old lady.

Without looking up, he spoke in a voice that was almost a whisper. "Lucia," he said, "it's just this once."

"No," she said. "No. I want my cake."

85 Maria began to cry. "Dios mio,"[13] she said. "My little girl."

Lorenzo leaned on his hands. "I'm sorry, Miss Mendez."

Maria turned to her. She was sobbing. "It's my daughter's birthday," she said. "How will she forgive me? Don't you have children?"

90 "I have three children," Lucia said. "And I never forgot their birthdays. I never had to rush out at the last minute."

"I was working," Maria said. "I'm all by myself with Teresa. I have to raise her alone."

"And whose fault is that?" Lucia waved at Lorenzo. "Pronto," 95 she said. "Box up my cake."[14]

Lorenzo eased the cake out of the display case and placed it into a white cardboard pastry box. His hands were soft and white. He drew a length of twine[15] from the dispenser, tied off the box, then snapped his wrists and broke the string from the leader.

100 Lucia put on her gloves. As she turned for the door Maria took her arm. "I'll beg you," she said. "Please, I'll buy the cake from you. I'll pay you ten dollars."

Lucia pulled her arm free. "I don't want your money."

"Twenty dollars, then." She pulled a folded bill from the pocket 105 of her dress and placed it in Lucia's hand. "Please, Mrs. Ronsavelli, take it."

Lucia tried to push the bill back into her hands, but Maria curled her fingers into fists and began to cry. "You can't do this," she said.

---

13 "Dios mio" "My God" (Spanish)
14 "Pronto...Box up my cake." "Put my cake in a box immediately."

15 a length of twine a piece of string

Lucia threw the crumpled bill to the floor and opened the door.
110 Maria fell to her knees and picked up the bill. "You witch!" she
screamed. "Puta! Whore!"[16]

Lucia did not look back. She moved slowly down Newbury
Street, being careful to avoid the spots of ice. What did that laundry
girl, or even Lorenzo, understand about her? What did they know
115 about devotion?[17]

From the alley behind her building she heard the screaming,
a terrible choked wail that rang from the street and into the alley
and echoed off the walls and trash cans. She imagined Maria the
laundress stumbling[18] home to her daughter, and she imagined the
120 red, contorted[19] face of the little girl when her friends arrived and
there was no cake.

Still, what would they know about suffering, even then? They
would know nothing. The light was poor in the staircase, and she
held the railing with her free hand. After each step she paused; she
125 let the flicker of pain[20] ease from her hips, then lifted again.

Inside the kitchen she raised the glass cover and took out last
week's cake. The air that had been under the glass smelled sweet
and ripe. The cake had not been touched; it might have been a clay
model of the new one. As she carried it to the trash, tips of chocolate
130 frosting broke off and scattered on the floor like shards of pottery.[21]

She swept up the pieces, washed the smudges of frosting[22]
from the cake stand with a sponge, then opened the bakery box,
removed the new cake and put it under the glass cover. It was dark
outside, and in the hills around the city the lights in the windows of
135 hundreds of houses glowed like the tiny white bulbs in the branches
of a Christmas tree. She thought of her children; they were up in
those hills, eating dinner with their own families—those little
light-skinned boys and girls who shrank from[23] their nana's[24] hugs,
kept their jackets on, and whispered to each other until it was time to
140 leave. It was cold near the window; she shivered and stepped away.

She sat at the kitchen table, beneath the photos of Nico and the
children. She looked at the door, wishing, as she did each time, that
there might be a knock, or that it might just swing open, and one of
them, just one of them, might be there.

---

16 **"Puta! Whore!"** woman who offers sex
   for money (Spanish, English)
17 **devotion** strong, loving loyalty
18 **stumbling** walking unsteadily
19 **contorted** in an unnatural shape
20 **flicker of pain** pain that comes and goes
   quickly

21 **shards of pottery** sharp pieces of broken
   dishes
22 **smudges of frosting** marks left by the
   sugary top of the cake
23 **shrank from** tried to get away from
24 **nana** grandmother (children's language)

FIRST READING

A Thinking About the Story

Discuss the following question with a partner.

> Did your feelings toward Lucia change as you read the story? Explain your answer.

B Understanding the Plot

Be prepared to answer the following questions with a partner or your class.

1. How is Lucia's health? Give details.
2. Who is Nico?
3. What is Lorenzo concerned about in lines 20–21?
4. What is Lucia's attitude toward the Puerto Ricans in her neighborhood? Explain why she feels this way.
5. Why does the priest think Lucia should consider moving to a nursing home?
6. Why does Maria need to ask Lucia for a favor?
7. Why doesn't Lorenzo bake a new cake for Maria's daughter?
8. What do we learn about Maria's life? Give details.
9. Why is Lucia hostile toward Maria's daughter? Give as many reasons as possible.
10. Why does Lucia get angry when Lorenzo calls her *Lucy*? (lines 56–60)
11. What do you think Lorenzo was about to say, but didn't? (lines 64–65)
12. How does Lucia view Maria's situation as a single mother?
13. To whom or what is Lucia devoted? (lines 114–115)
14. What does Lucia do with the cake she buys each week?
15. Where do Lucia's children and grandchildren live? Does she see them often?

PART 2

CRITICAL THINKING

A Exploring Themes

Reread "The Birthday Cake." Then answer the following questions, which explore the story more deeply.

1. Why does Lucia buy the same cake each week?
2. In what ways is Lorenzo different from Lucia?

3. Describe the ways in which Lucia is isolated from her family and her community. How does this influence her behavior?

4. Lucia often doesn't say out loud what she is thinking. Give some examples of her private thoughts. Say what they reveal about her character.

B Analyzing Style

SETTING AND ATMOSPHERE

The **setting** of a story is the place where the events occur. It also includes the time period and the social environment. Setting contributes to **atmosphere**, which is the feeling we get about the characters and their surroundings. For example, if a scene is set in a dark street at night in a dangerous city, the atmosphere may be filled with tension and fear.

The story begins as Lucia makes her way slowly and painfully through her working-class neighborhood. The image of light *draining from the sky* (line 1) helps set the scene (it is the end of the day). It also contributes to the atmosphere (there is a sad feeling about the disappearing light). When Lucia enters the bakery and finds Lorenzo anxiously waiting for her, the atmosphere changes from sadness to tension. We start to feel worried about what will happen next.

Exercise 1

There are three settings in "The Birthday Cake." Write them on the lines below.

1. _____

2. _____

3. _____

Exercise 2

Answer the following questions.

1. Lucia's neighborhood is full of loud noises. Give examples. Explain how these sounds contribute to the atmosphere.

2. In the bakery scene, how does the author create an atmosphere of rising tension?

3. How is the cake described in lines 126–133? Pay attention to the image of the frosting on the floor, as well as to how the cake looks and smells in its container. How does the description of the cake reflect the atmosphere in Lucia's kitchen?

4. At the end of the story, Lucia looks at the hills around the city where her family lives. How do the hills seem different from her own neighborhood? How does the contrast between the two neighborhoods help us understand Lucia better?

5. Find at least two references to weather in the story. How do they contribute to the atmosphere?

C Judging for Yourself

Express yourself as personally as you like in your answers to the following questions.

1. Which woman do you think Lorenzo should have sold the cake to?

2. In your view, should Lucia move to a place where older people can receive special care, such as a nursing home? Explain your answer.

3. To what extent do you think Maria is responsible for her daughter's disappointing birthday?

4. Do you sympathize with Lucia's anger and concern about the changes in her neighborhood?

D Making Connections

Answer the following questions in a small group.

1. Is immigration a controversial issue in your country? What sorts of tensions arise between immigrants and native-born people in your country, or between different immigrant groups?

2. In your community, is it common to hear more than one language? If so, which ones are spoken? Does this create any problems?

3. Are single parents common in your society? How are they regarded? Does anyone help them raise their children?

4. How are birthdays celebrated in your country? Are there any special foods, gifts, or rituals?

E Debate

Decide whether you are for or against the following statement. Write several arguments that support your view. Share your points with a classmate who has taken the opposite position.

Immigration is good for a country.

PART 3

GRAMMAR IN CONTEXT

PARALLEL STRUCTURE

Coordinating conjunctions such as *and, or*, and *but* connect two or more parts of a sentence. These parts can be words, phrases, or whole clauses. A general principle of clear writing is that the connected parts should have the same grammatical form. This is referred to as **parallel structure**.

- Coordinating conjunctions can join two or more words that are the same part of speech. For example, they can connect two adjectives or two nouns.

    *His hands were <u>soft</u> **and** <u>white</u>.* (line 97)

    *"I could give you some <u>sugar cookies</u>," he said. "**Or** some <u>cannolis</u>."* (lines 61–62)

    *This Maria from the laundry had <u>a child</u> **but** <u>no husband</u>.* (line 33)

- Coordinating conjunctions can join two or more gerunds or infinitives. When joining infinitives, the second *to* is often omitted.

    *Lucia's doctor had warned her against <u>getting angry</u> **or** <u>walking too much</u>.*

    *Lucia was too upset <u>to eat</u> **or** <u>drink</u> anything.*

- Coordinating conjunctions can join two or more prepositional phrases.

    *She heard a terrible choked wail that rang <u>from the street</u> **and** <u>into the alley</u>.* (adapted from lines 116–118)

- Coordinating conjunctions can join two or more clauses. When two independent clauses have different subjects, place a comma after the first clause.

    *<u>Her legs were thick now</u>, **and** <u>her hips hurt each day</u>.*

    When two independent clauses have the same subject, you may omit the subject the second time and leave out the comma.

    *<u>Lucia removed her leather gloves</u> **and** <u>put them into her purse</u>.* (line 36)

- A common mistake is to join elements that aren't parallel using a coordinating conjunction.

    Not parallel: *Lorenzo likes <u>to bake</u> cakes **and** <u>helping</u> people in the neighborhood.*

    Parallel: *Lorenzo likes <u>baking</u> cakes **and** <u>helping</u> people in the neighborhood.*

    Parallel: *Lorenzo likes <u>to bake</u> cakes **and** <u>to help</u> people in the neighborhood.*

Exercise 1

In each of the following sentences, the coordinating conjunction is in bold and the two parallel parts are underlined. Write the grammatical structure of the two underlined parts. The first one is done for you.

1. Each week Lucia bought <u>a cake</u> **but** <u>no cookies</u> from the bakery.

two nouns

2. Lorenzo finished <u>cleaning</u> his equipment **and** <u>counting</u> his money.
_____

3. <u>Maria wanted to bake a cake for her daughter</u>, **but** <u>she didn't have time</u>.
_____

4. Lucia wanted her family <u>to visit</u> her **or** <u>to invite</u> her over more often.
_____

5. The <u>kind</u> **and** <u>understanding</u> priest was concerned about Lucia.
_____

6. Many Puerto Ricans <u>moved to Lucia's neighborhood</u> **and** <u>quickly found jobs</u>. _____

Exercise 2

Look at the following sentences from the story. In each sentence, circle the coordinating conjunction and underline the parallel parts. There may be more than one coordinating conjunction and several parallel parts in each sentence.

1. She stopped by a bench, wanting to sit but knowing that she shouldn't. (adapted from lines 12–14)

2. He had already cleaned his equipment and put away his flour and eggs and sugar. (adapted from lines 69–70)

3. She thought of Nico, how when he lay sick in bed during his last days she had gone outside and asked the children not to make noise… (lines 78–80)

4. What did that laundry girl, or even Lorenzo, understand about her? (lines 113–114)

5. She looked at the door, wishing that there might be a knock or that it might just swing open. (adapted from lines 142–144)

Exercise 3

The following sentences are not written with parallel structure. Rewrite them correctly.

1. Lucia loved to speak Italian and cooking Italian food.

2. Maria's hands were rough, but looking clean.

3. Lorenzo can't decide whether to please Lucia or he should please Maria.

4. Lucia disliked the Puerto Ricans and to give up her cake.

5. Don't go to that bakery or eating at that restaurant.

6. Remember your daughter's birthday and buying her a present.

7. Teresa screamed angrily and loud.

8. Maria does not buy a cake or to bake one.

Exercise 4

Complete the following sentences using parallel structure. Compare your answers with a partner.

1. My mother bought me pretty shoes and _____.

2. I would like to go to a movie or _____.

3. It was late, but _____.

4. I visited Peru and _____ during my vacation.

5. You shouldn't be rude or _____ to your boss.

6. People need clean air and _____ to be healthy.

7. We always go swimming and _____ in our free time.

8. You should stay in the house or _____.

9. Young children like to run and _____.

10. The house survived the earthquake but _____.

PART 4 VOCABULARY BUILDING

PREPOSITIONS OF PLACE

"The Birthday Cake" has many **prepositions of place**. These prepositions indicate where something is located. For example, we learn that Maria works *at the laundry* (line 43), that there is fruit *in the carts* (line 2), and that there are people *on the sidewalk* (line 29).

Knowing when to use *at*, *on*, or *in* is tricky. As a general rule, we use *at* to show a specific place or point: *at the store, at the traffic light*; we use *on* to indicate a surface: *on the floor, on the desk*; and we use *in* when there is a confined space: *in the park, in the building*.

There are special rules for using *at*, *on*, and *in* to give an address:

> *I live **at** 145 Sunset Boulevard.* (specific address)

> *I live **on** Sunset Boulevard.* (street)

I live *in* Los Angeles. (city)

I live *in* California. (state)

I live *in* the United States. (country)

Other common prepositions of place include *behind* (line 20), *near* (line 140), *under* (line 133), *between*, and *above*.

Exercise 1

Complete each of the following sentences with the correct preposition of place: *at, on, in, above, behind, between, near,* or *under*.

1. Lucia lives _____ a rapidly changing neighborhood.

2. She sat down _____ the bench to rest her legs.

3. Lucia had trouble keeping the floor _____ her kitchen table clean.

4. Nico and Lucia lived _____ a busy street for many years.

5. "Don't come _____ my tomatoes again," Lucia warned Teresa.

6. Lorenzo stood _____ Lucia and Maria to separate the two women.

7. Nico lay _____ three blankets, but he still couldn't get warm.

8. Lorenzo stopped _____ 12 Elm Street to deliver a cake.

9. It was cold _____ the room, so Lucia closed the window.

10. The sky _____ Lucia's head was full of dark clouds.

11. Maria heard a noise _____ her and turned her head around to look.

12. Lucia was born _____ Italy.

WORDS WITH NEGATIVE CONNOTATIONS

"The Birthday Cake" is a story filled with sadness and anger. To create this atmosphere, the author uses many words with **negative connotations**. The connotations of a word are its associations. Connotation is often contrasted with denotation, which refers to a word's dictionary definition.

In the first paragraph, there is an *odor* (line 4) in the street. An odor is literally a smell. However, the word *odor* has the more specific connotation of an unpleasant smell. When referring to something that smells good, such as a flower or freshly baked bread, we would probably use *scent* or *aroma* instead. These words have a positive connotation. By learning the connotations of words, you will become better at choosing the most appropriate word for a situation.

Exercise 2

Match each word in the left-hand column to its denotation (dictionary definition) in the right-hand column.

_____ **1.** drain (line 1)	**a.** worried
_____ **2.** rotten (line 2)	**b.** shake
_____ **3.** sour (line 3)	**c.** bent out of shape
_____ **4.** unpleasant (line 3)	**d.** disappear slowly
_____ **5.** spoil (line 9)	**e.** having a sharp taste
_____ **6.** sore (line 11)	**f.** loud cry
_____ **7.** concerned (line 21)	**g.** offensive
_____ **8.** wail (line 117)	**h.** ruin
_____ **9.** contorted (line 120)	**i.** decayed
_____ **10.** shiver (line 140)	**j.** painful

Exercise 3

The following sentence pairs use each word in Exercise 2 in two different contexts. Complete each sentence pair with the same word.

1. a. If it rains, it will _____ the picnic.

    b. Some people think that cooking a steak for too long will _____ the flavor.

2. a. The singer canceled her concert because of a _____ throat.

    b. After getting a shot from the doctor, my arm was _____ for days.

3. **a.** Many people around the world are very _____ about global warming.

   b. Why are you _____ about your daughter? She is the best student in her class.

4. **a.** I was holding my boyfriend's hand at the horror movie, and I felt him _____ at a scary moment.

   b. When I walked home in the snow without a coat, I quickly started to _____.

5. **a.** The water wouldn't _____ from my broken bathtub.

   b. A long day at work will always _____ my energy.

6. **a.** This dish needs more sweetness to balance the _____ flavor.

   b. My friend's _____ personality improved when he met his new girlfriend.

7. **a.** Letting fruit become _____ is a waste of money.

   b. I don't think society made him a criminal. I think he was _____ from the start.

8. **a.** I'm sorry you found the party so _____. I didn't realize your ex-husband would be there.

   b. Having the flu was extremely _____, but I'm feeling better now.

9. **a.** It's hard to ignore the _____ of a baby, but it doesn't always mean that something is wrong.

   b. I hope I never hear the _____ of an angry ghost!

10. **a.** The politician's explanation for his behavior was so _____ that it was impossible to believe.

    b. The yoga teacher _____ her body into an incredible position.

Exercise 4

Use each word in the left-hand column of Exercise 2 to complete the following paragraph.

Lucia was _____ about the changes in her neighborhood. Life wasn't easy for her these days. Parts of her body were always _____. As she walked to the bakery, the cold wind made her _____. She saw some _____ fruit lying on the sidewalk. At the bakery, she refused to let Maria have the cake. The laundress gave a

_____, and her face became _____

with worry and rage. Lucia walked home slowly. Why had she let Lorenzo

and Maria _____ her day? In the kitchen, she took out

some milk, but it smelled _____. The events of the day

brought back many _____ memories. As she thought

about her family in the hills, the color started to _____

from her face.

PART 5

WRITING ACTIVITIES

1. Imagine you are a newspaper reporter in Lucia's city. Choose one of the
   characters from "The Birthday Cake" to interview about the relationship
   between Italians and Puerto Ricans in the community. Write five
   questions to ask your character. Then write a complete answer to each
   question. For example, a question for Lorenzo might be, *Do you have
   Puerto Rican friends?*

2. Find a short article about immigrants in your country. Sources could
   include a newspaper, a magazine, or the Internet. Summarize the article.
   Say whether the writer expresses an opinion about the subject. Try to
   use several different prepositions of place in your response.

3. Choose a birthday that was special in some way. It could be your own
   birthday or someone else's, and it could be a positive memory or a
   negative one. Describe the setting and explain what happened. Try to
   use descriptive imagery to re-create the atmosphere of the event.

4. Both "The Birthday Cake" and "Transition" have a grandmother as the
   main character. Contrast the personalities of the two grandmothers and
   the relationship that each one has with her family.

12 The Kiss

Kate Chopin
(1851–1904)

Kate Chopin was born in St. Louis, Missouri. Her mother's family was French-Creole, and her father's family was Irish. Chopin's father died when she was very young, and she grew up surrounded by several generations of strong women. Many of her stories deal with women searching for freedom from male control, a theme that was ahead of its time. Chopin wrote over a hundred short stories. Her two major collections were *Bayou Folk* (1894) and *A Night in Acadie* (1897). Some of her most well-known stories include "Désirée's Baby" and "The Story of an Hour." Her short novel *The Awakening* (1899) dealt with the controversial subjects of women's sexuality and unhappiness in marriage. *The Awakening* was criticized as immoral and publicly condemned. As a result, Chopin wrote very little toward the end of her life. Today she is regarded as a master of the short-story form.

The Kiss

A confident young woman finds that her plans for the future are suddenly in danger.

It was still quite light out of doors, but inside with the curtains drawn[1] and the smouldering[2] fire sending out a dim, uncertain glow, the room was full of deep shadows.

Brantain sat in one of these shadows; it had overtaken him and he did not mind. The obscurity[3] lent him courage to keep his eyes fastened as ardently[4] as he liked upon the girl who sat in the firelight.

She was very handsome, with a certain fine, rich coloring that belongs to the healthy brune[5] type. She was quite composed,[6] as she idly stroked the satiny coat of the cat that lay curled in her lap, and she occasionally sent a slow glance into the shadow where her companion sat. They were talking low, of indifferent[7] things which plainly were not the things that occupied their thoughts. She knew that he loved her—a frank, blustering fellow[8] without guile enough[9] to conceal his feelings, and no desire to do so. For two weeks past he had sought her society[10] eagerly and persistently. She was confidently waiting for him to declare himself[11] and she meant to accept him. The rather insignificant and unattractive Brantain was enormously rich; and she liked and required the entourage which wealth could give her.[12]

During one of the pauses between their talk of the last tea and the next reception the door opened and a young man entered whom Brantain knew quite well. The girl turned her face toward him. A stride or two brought him to her side, and bending over her chair—before she could suspect his intention, for she did not realize that he had not seen her visitor—he pressed an ardent, lingering kiss upon her lips.

Brantain slowly arose; so did the girl arise, but quickly, and the newcomer stood between them, a little amusement and some defiance[13] struggling with the confusion in his face.

---

1 **drawn** closed (used for curtains)
2 **smouldering** slow-burning
3 **obscurity** difficulty being seen
4 **ardently** passionately
5 **brune** brown-haired (usually *brunette*)
6 **She was quite composed.** She appeared confident and relaxed.
7 **indifferent** unimportant
8 **a frank, blustering fellow** someone who says what he thinks and feels
9 **without guile enough** without the ability to deceive
10 **sought her society** tried to spend time with her
11 **declare himself** propose marriage
12 **the entourage which wealth could give her** the servants and good lifestyle that money would provide
13 **defiance** open resistance

"I believe," stammered Brantain, "I see that I have stayed too long. I—I had no idea—that is, I must wish you good-by." He was clutching his hat with both hands, and probably did not perceive that she was extending her hand to him, her presence of mind had not completely deserted her; but she could not have trusted herself to speak.

"Hang me if I saw him sitting there,[14] Nattie! I know it's deuced awkward[15] for you. But I hope you'll forgive me this once—this very first break.[16] Why, what's the matter?"

"Don't touch me; don't come near me," she returned angrily. "What do you mean by entering the house without ringing?"

"I came in with your brother, as I often do," he answered coldly, in self-justification. "We came in the side way. He went upstairs and I came in here hoping to find you. The explanation is simple enough and ought to satisfy you that the misadventure[17] was unavoidable. But do say that you forgive me, Nathalie," he entreated, softening.

"Forgive you! You don't know what you are talking about. Let me pass. It depends upon—a good deal whether I ever forgive you."

At that next reception which she and Brantain had been talking about she approached the young man with a delicious frankness of manner[18] when she saw him there.

"Will you let me speak to you a moment or two, Mr. Brantain?" she asked with an engaging but perturbed smile.[19] He seemed extremely unhappy; but when she took his arm and walked away with him, seeking a retired corner,[20] a ray of hope mingled with the almost comical misery of his expression. She was apparently very outspoken.[21]

"Perhaps I should not have sought this interview, Mr. Brantain; but—but, oh, I have been very uncomfortable, almost miserable since that little encounter the other afternoon. When I thought how you might have misinterpreted it, and believed things"—hope was plainly gaining the ascendancy over misery[22] in Brantain's round, guileless

---

14 **"Hang me if I saw him sitting there"** "I really didn't see him sitting there." (old-fashioned slang)

15 **deuced awkward** extremely uncomfortable (old-fashioned expression)

16 **this very first break** the first time I have been careless

17 **misadventure** unlucky event

18 **delicious frankness of manner** delightfully honest behavior

19 **an engaging but perturbed smile** an attractive but anxious smile

20 **a retired corner** a private place in the room

21 **outspoken** willing to speak openly without hesitation

22 **hope was plainly gaining the ascendancy over misery** he was becoming more hopeful and less unhappy

face—"Of course, I know it is nothing to you, but for my own sake I do want you to understand that Mr. Harvy is an intimate friend of long standing.[23] Why, we have always been like cousins—like brother and sister, I may say. He is my brother's most intimate associate and
65 often fancies that he is entitled to the same privileges as the family. Oh, I know it is absurd,[24] uncalled for, to tell you this; undignified even," she was almost weeping, "but it makes so much difference to me what you think of—of me." Her voice had grown very low and agitated. The misery had all disappeared from Brantain's face.

70 "Then you do really care what I think, Miss Nathalie? May I call you Miss Nathalie?" They turned into a long, dim corridor that was lined on either side with tall, graceful plants. They walked slowly to the very end of it. When they turned to retrace their steps Brantain's face was radiant and hers was triumphant.[25]

75 Harvy was among the guests at the wedding; and he sought her out in a rare moment when she stood alone.

"Your husband," he said, smiling, "has sent me over to kiss you."

A quick blush suffused her face and round polished throat.[26] "I suppose it's natural for a man to feel and act generously on an
80 occasion of this kind. He tells me he doesn't want his marriage to interrupt wholly that pleasant intimacy which has existed between you and me. I don't know what you've been telling him," with an insolent[27] smile, "but he has sent me here to kiss you."

She felt like a chess player who, by the clever handling of his
85 pieces, sees the game taking the course intended. Her eyes were bright and tender with a smile as they glanced up into his; and her lips looked hungry for the kiss which they invited.

"But, you know," he went on quietly, "I didn't tell him so, it would have seemed ungrateful, but I can tell you. I've stopped
90 kissing women; it's dangerous."

Well, she had Brantain and his million left. A person can't have everything in this world; and it was a little unreasonable of her to expect it.

---

23 **an intimate friend of long standing** a close friend for a long time
24 **absurd** ridiculous
25 **Brantain's face was radiant and hers was triumphant.** Brantain's face expressed joy and hers expressed victory.

26 **a quick blush suffused her face and round polished throat** her face and neck suddenly turned very red
27 **insolent** lacking respect

FIRST READING

A Thinking About the Story

Discuss the following question with a partner.

> Does any character get what he or she wants by the end of the story? Explain your answer.

B Understanding the Plot

Be prepared to answer the following questions with a partner or your class.

1. Why is Brantain happy to sit in the dark? (lines 4–6)
2. What is Nathalie confident about in lines 15–16? Is her confidence justified?
3. What does Nathalie think about Brantain's physical appearance and his personality? (lines 12–19)
4. Why is Nathalie interested in Brantain?
5. What is Nathalie's relationship with Harvy? Give details to support your answer.
6. Why does Brantain get up to leave? (lines 29–34)
7. How does Harvy feel when he realizes what has happened? How does he explain his mistake?
8. When Nathalie tells Harvy that her forgiveness *depends upon—a good deal*, what does she mean? (lines 45–46) Explain your answer.
9. When she next sees Brantain, how does Nathalie explain the kiss between Harvy and herself? Is Brantain satisfied by Nathalie's explanation?
10. What does Brantain tell Harvy to do at the wedding? Why does he make this suggestion?
11. How does Nathalie react when she hears about Brantain's suggestion?
12. What does Harvy decide to do about Brantain's suggestion?
13. What is Nathalie's state of mind at the end of the story?

PART 2

CRITICAL THINKING

A Exploring Themes

Reread "The Kiss." Then answer the following questions, which explore the story more deeply.

1. "The Kiss" presents Nathalie as a complex character. Discuss how Nathalie's personality cannot be easily categorized as completely good or completely bad.

2. How does the sentence "Brantain's face was *radiant* and hers was *triumphant*" reflect the different personalities of Brantain and Nathalie? (lines 73–74)

3. How does money shape the lives of the characters in "The Kiss"?

4. Why do you think Harvy chooses not to kiss Nathalie at the end of the story?

B Analyzing Style

THIRD-PERSON POINT OF VIEW

When a story is told from a **third-person point of view**, the narrator describes the action using the pronouns *he*, *she*, and *they*. Often the narrator is not a part of the action and remains invisible.

Sometimes a third-person narrator only portrays the characters from the outside, so our perspective is limited to their actions. Other times the narrator can see into the mind of one or more characters, so we get a direct look at their thoughts. In "The Kiss," the narration leads us to see events mostly from Nathalie's point of view.

Exercise 1

Answer the following questions.

1. When the story opens, we experience the events from Brantain's point of view. What is he thinking?

2. Give at least two places in the story where we are directly told what Nathalie is thinking. What do we learn from these thoughts?

3. Harvy is shown entirely from the outside. We are not given access to his thoughts. How does this affect our understanding of him?

IRONY

Irony is a difficult literary concept. It refers to a contrast between appearance and reality. Irony takes three main forms. In all three forms, something important is invisible to at least one of the characters. The truth of the situation lies beneath the surface.

- In one form of irony, a character says something that seems to mean one thing but that really means something very different.

- In another form, a character expects one thing to happen, but in fact the opposite occurs.
- In a third form, we know something important that a character in the story doesn't know.

Irony is central to the scene in which Nathalie explains the kiss to Brantain. When Brantain sees the kiss at the beginning of the story, he correctly infers that Nathalie and Harvy are lovers. Nathalie then tries to deceive him by saying that he "might have misinterpreted it, and believed things" (lines 58–59). She convinces Brantain that she and Harvy are just friends. The irony is that Brantain's original interpretation was correct. We know that Nathalie has made him believe a lie instead.

Exercise 2

Answer the following questions.

1. Nathalie tells Brantain that "it makes so much difference to me what you think of—of me." (lines 67–68) What does Nathalie want Brantain to think she cares about? What does she really care about?
2. What does Brantain not understand (but we do) when he sends Harvy over to kiss Nathalie at the wedding?
3. Nathalie thinks of herself as a clever chess player about to win her game (lines 84–85). What does winning mean to Nathalie? Do her expectations come true?

C Judging for Yourself

Express yourself as personally as you like in your answers to the following questions.

1. Overall, were you sympathetic to Nathalie? Did you want her to succeed? Explain your answer.
2. What do you think of Nathalie's decision to marry Brantain for his money?
3. Do you think Nathalie and Brantain will have a happy marriage? Explain your answer.

D Making Connections

Answer the following questions in a small group.

1. In your country, what do people look for when choosing a husband or a wife? Does your generation view this question differently from previous generations?

2. Do most people want to get married in your country today? Discuss some of the pros and cons of marriage for men and women.

3. Is being faithful (not cheating) considered essential to a successful relationship in your country? Are there different standards for men and for women?

E Debate

Decide whether you are for or against the following statement. Write several arguments that support your view. Share your points with a classmate who has taken the opposite position.

People should marry for love.

PART 3

GRAMMAR IN CONTEXT

ADVERB FORMATION

An **adverb** is a part of speech that modifies a verb, an adjective, or another adverb. Kate Chopin frequently uses adverbs to convey the emotions and motivations of her characters.

Many adverbs are formed from adjectives in the following ways.

- A common way to form an adverb is to add *–ly* to an adjective—for example, *plainly* (line 12), *completely* (line 33), *really* (line 70).
- If an adjective ends in a consonant followed by *–y*, change the *–y* to *–i* before adding *–ly*. For example, *angry* becomes *angrily* (line 38).
- If an adjective ends in *–ic*, add *–ally*—for example, *sympathetically*. The adjective *public* is an exception and becomes *publicly* as an adverb.
- If an adjective ends with a consonant followed by *–le*, drop the *–e* and add *–y*. For example, *idle* becomes *idly* (line 9).

Exercise 1

Work with a partner. Using the rules in the explanation on adverb formation, write the corresponding adverb for each adjective. Do not use a dictionary.

1. uncertain (line 2)
2. awkward (line 36)
3. unhappy (line 52)
4. comical (line 54)
5. uncomfortable (line 57)
6. guileless (line 60)
7. intimate (line 62)
8. graceful (line 72)
9. hungry (line 87)
10. dangerous (line 90)

ADVERB PLACEMENT

The rules for adverb placement in English are complicated. Some adverbs have a fixed position, while others can be used in more than one place in a sentence. The following guidelines cover some of the basic issues of adverb placement.

The adverb type determines its placement in the sentence. Five common types of adverbs are *degree, frequency, manner, place,* and *time.*

- Adverbs of **degree** answer the question *how much.* They go directly before the word they modify and give it a stronger or weaker meaning.

    *It was still **quite** light out of doors...* (line 1)

    *He seemed **extremely** unhappy.* (lines 51–52)

- Adverbs of **frequency** answer the question *how often.* They usually go between the subject and the verb.

    *She **occasionally** glanced at her companion.* (adapted from line 10)

    *"I came in with your brother, as I **often** do," he answered...* (line 40)

When there is an auxiliary verb, adverbs of frequency usually go between the auxiliary and the main verb.

    *"We have **always** been like cousins," Nathalie said.* (adapted from line 63)

Sometimes an adverb of frequency can be placed at the beginning or end of a sentence.

    ***Sometimes** bad things happen to good people.*

    *Do you come here **often**?*

- Adverbs of **manner** answer the question *in what way.* They are usually placed after the verb.

    *"Don't touch me; don't come near me," she returned **angrily**.* (line 38)

If the verb is transitive, the adverb goes after the object. Do not place an adverb between a verb and its object.

    *For the past two weeks he had pursued her **eagerly** and **persistently**.* (adapted from lines 14–15)

- Adverbs of **place** answer the question *where.* They go after the verb.

    *He went **upstairs**.* (line 41)

If the verb is transitive, the adverb goes after the object.

    *The young man was at the reception. She approached him **there**.* (adapted from lines 47–49)

- Adverbs of **time** answer the question *when.* They generally go at the end of a clause.

    *Nathalie saw Brantain **yesterday**.*

    *I'm sure that Nathalie will feel better **soon**.*

Exercise 2

Underline each adverb in the following sentences and write what type of adverb it is. Use the placement of the adverb to help you decide. The first one is done for you as an example.

     (frequency)   *(manner)*   *(degree)*

1. "I can <u>never</u> marry you," Nathalie said <u>angrily</u> to Harvy. "I'm <u>extremely</u> tired of saying this."
2. Nathalie thought Harvy would love her forever. She hoped they would often see each other after her marriage.
3. After seeing the kiss, Brantain was enormously unhappy and ran downstairs.
4. Nathalie always got what she wanted. It was a strange experience to be very unsure of her future.
5. Nathalie was quite nervous when she approached Brantain quickly.
6. Brantain smiled radiantly after talking to Nathalie.
7. Nathalie thought her plan had worked perfectly, so she was wholly unprepared for Harvy's rejection.
8. Nathalie badly wanted Harvy to kiss her, but thoughts of Brantain's fortune soon improved her mood.

Exercise 3

Place the adverb in parentheses in the correct position in the sentence. If there is more than one option, choose only one. Share your answers with a partner.

1. "I can marry you," Nathalie said to Harvy. (never)
2. "I'm unhappy," she sighed. (extremely)
3. Harvy entered the house. (downstairs)
4. Nathalie will marry Brantain. (tomorrow)
5. Brantain listened to Nathalie's explanation of the kiss. (eagerly)
6. Nathalie thought she had planned everything, so she was surprised by Harvy's rejection. (perfectly)
7. Harvy wished that he'd been able to marry Nathalie. (occasionally)
8. Nathalie smiled when she saw her beautiful new house. (radiantly)
9. Brantain was kind to Harvy after the wedding. (quite)
10. Nathalie saw Brantain. (outside)

Exercise 4

Write a short paragraph that includes the following adverbs: *frequently, outside, very, today,* and *quietly.* Make sure you place each adverb in its correct position in the sentence.

PART 4

VOCABULARY BUILDING

ADJECTIVES DESCRIBING EMOTIONS

Kate Chopin shows us the changing emotions of Nathalie and Brantain in "The Kiss." She uses a careful choice of **adjectives** to help us understand the characters. For example, when we first meet Nathalie, she is described as *composed* (line 8). This adjective means *calm* and is a perfect description of her as a confident young woman. However, when the kiss threatens her plans, her confidence is shaken. She becomes *perturbed* (line 51), which means *anxious*.

Exercise 1

Look at the following adjectives from the story. Match each adjective to its definition in the right-hand column.

_____ **1.** uncertain (line 2)	**a.** not thankful
_____ **2.** frank (line 13)	**b.** loving
_____ **3.** awkward (line 36)	**c.** not rational
_____ **4.** miserable (line 57)	**d.** not confident
_____ **5.** triumphant (line 74)	**e.** honest
_____ **6.** tender (line 86)	**f.** uncomfortable
_____ **7.** ungrateful (line 89)	**g.** successful
_____ **8.** unreasonable (line 92)	**h.** very unhappy

Exercise 2

Complete the following sentences with appropriate adjectives from the left-hand list in Exercise 1.

1. Harvy didn't mean to create an _____ situation on the day he visited Nathalie's house.

2. Seeing the kiss suddenly made Brantain _____ about Nathalie's feelings.

3. Nathalie was _____ when she thought she had lost Brantain.

4. Brantain started to suspect that Nathalie had not been _____ with him.

5. Nathalie felt _____ when she realized her plan to marry Brantain had worked.

6. On her wedding day, Nathalie's expression showed that she still had _____ feelings for Harvy.

7. At the end of the story, Nathalie tried to convince herself it was _____ to want both Brantain and Harvy.

8. Nathalie was _____ for Harvy's decision to do the right thing.

Exercise 3

Look at the following sentences. Write true (T) or false (F) according to the plot of the story. Explain your answers to a partner.

1. Nathalie had tender feelings for Brantain. (　)
2. When he noticed that Brantain was in the room, Harvy felt very awkward. (　)
3. Harvy thought Nathalie was being unreasonable in blaming him for the kiss. (　)
4. Brantain seemed ungrateful when Nathalie started talking to him at the reception. (　)
5. Nathalie was frank with Brantain about her relationship with Harvy. (　)
6. Brantain was uncertain whether Nathalie had told him the truth. (　)
7. When Harvy said that he'd been sent to kiss her, Nathalie felt triumphant. (　)
8. Nathalie was miserable at the end of the story. (　)

Exercise 4

Choose five of the words from the left-hand column in Exercise 1. Write a dialogue between Brantain and Nathalie that includes those five words.

PART 5 # WRITING ACTIVITIES

1. "The Kiss" was written over a hundred years ago. Still, it is easy for us to relate to the characters in the story. Choose a person from an older generation to interview about what it was like to get married in his or her time. Prepare at least three questions in advance. Possible questions might include the way people met their husbands and wives, the issues that were considered most important, and the age at which people usually got married. Write several paragraphs about what you learn from your interview. Conclude with your own opinion about how getting married today compares with getting married in the past. Try to include a variety of adverbs in your writing.

2. Marrying for money is a frequently explored theme. In the novel *Pride and Prejudice* by Jane Austen, a family has a serious problem that can be solved if one of the five daughters marries a rich man. The song "Gold Digger" by Kanye West, the American rapper, warns against women who chase rich men. And the television series *Downton Abbey* (2011) features a British aristocrat who marries a rich American woman

for her money, although he later grows to love her. Write a report on a work you know that deals with this subject. Summarize the work and describe its attitude toward marrying for money. Say whether you agree or disagree with the attitude presented.

3. "The Kiss" and "Some Thing Blue" (pages 114–115) are both stories about women marrying for reasons other than love. Write a short essay comparing these two stories. First, explain the reason that each woman decides to get married. Next, compare and contrast the personalities of the two women and their mood at the end of the two stories. In your conclusion, say whether you think either woman made the right decision.

PATHS TO ADULTHOOD

Letter to Mama
The Last Word Was Love
Girl
Ambush

13 ～ Letter to Mama

Armistead Maupin
(b. 1944)

Armistead Maupin grew up in North Carolina. He served in the U.S. Navy during the Vietnam War and later became a journalist. In 1971, Maupin moved to San Francisco. He began writing a series of stories about life in his new city. The stories, called *Tales of the City*, quickly became popular. They have been expanded into nine novels and made into a successful television program. The final book in the series, *The Days of Anna Madrigal*, was published in 2014. A musical version opened in San Francisco in 2011. Maupin's stories portray the changing lives of his characters and the evolving culture of San Francisco with humor and warmth.

Letter to Mama

A young man reveals a long-kept secret.

Dear Mama,

    I'm sorry it's taken me so long to write. Every time I try to write to you and Papa I realize I'm not saying the things that are in my heart. That would be O.K., if I loved you any less than I do, but you are still my parents and I am still your child.

    I have friends who think I'm foolish to write this letter. I hope they're wrong. I hope their doubts are based on parents who loved and trusted them less than mine do. I hope especially that you'll see this as an act of love on my part, a sign of my continuing need to share my life with you. I wouldn't have written, I guess, if you hadn't told me about your involvement in the Save Our Children campaign.[1] That, more than anything, made it clear that my responsibility was to tell you the truth, that your own child is homosexual, and that I never needed saving from anything except the cruel and ignorant[2] piety[3] of people like Anita Bryant.

    I'm sorry, Mama. Not for what I am, but for how you must feel at this moment. I know what that feeling is, for I felt it for most of my life. Revulsion,[4] shame, disbelief—rejection through fear of something I knew, even as a child, was as basic to my nature as the color of my eyes.

    No, Mama, I wasn't "recruited."[5] No seasoned[6] homosexual ever served as my mentor.[7] But you know what? I wish someone had. I wish someone older than me and wiser than the people in Orlando had taken me aside[8] and said, "You're all right, kid. You can grow up to be a doctor or a teacher just like anyone else. You're not crazy or sick or evil. You can succeed and be happy and find peace with friends—all kinds of friends—who don't give a damn[9] *who* you go to bed with. Most of all, though, you can love and be loved, without hating yourself for it."

    But no one ever said that to me, Mama. I had to find it out on my own, with the help of the city that has become my home. I know this may be hard for you to believe, but San Francisco is full of men and

---

1 **Save Our Children campaign** a campaign to prevent the hiring of gay teachers in the late 1970s headed by Anita Bryant, a conservative Christian
2 **ignorant** lacking knowledge or awareness
3 **piety** religious faith

4 **revulsion** horror
5 **recruited** persuaded to join a group
6 **seasoned** experienced
7 **mentor** trusted advisor or teacher
8 **taken me aside** spoken to me privately
9 **don't give a damn** don't care at all (informal)

women, both straight and gay,[10] who don't consider sexuality in measuring the worth of another human being.

35   These aren't radicals[11] or weirdos,[12] Mama. They are shop clerks and bankers and little old ladies and people who nod and smile to you when you meet them on the bus. Their attitude is neither patronizing[13] nor pitying. And their message is so simple: Yes, you are a person. Yes, I like you. Yes, it's all right for you to like me, too.

40   I know what you must be thinking now. You're asking yourself: What did we do wrong? How did we let this happen? Which one of us made him that way?

I can't answer that, Mama. In the long run,[14] I guess I really don't care. All I know is this: If you and Papa are responsible for the
45 way I am, then I thank you with all my heart,[15] for it's the light and the joy of my life.

I know I can't tell you what it is to be gay. But I can tell you what it's not.

It's not hiding behind words, Mama. Like family and decency
50 and Christianity. It's not fearing your body, or the pleasures that God made for it. It's not judging your neighbor, except when he's crass[16] or unkind.

Being gay has taught me tolerance, compassion and humility.[17] It has shown me the limitless possibilities of living. It has given me
55 people whose passion and kindness and sensitivity have provided a constant source of strength.

It has brought me into the family of man,[18] Mama, and I like it here. I *like* it.

There's not much else I can say, except that I'm the same Michael
60 you've always known. You just know me better now. I have never consciously done anything to hurt you. I never will.

Please don't feel you have to answer this right away. It's enough for me to know that I no longer have to lie to the people who taught me to value the truth.

65   Mary Ann[19] sends her love.
Everything is fine at 28 Barbary Lane.

Your loving son,
Michael

---

10 **straight and gay** heterosexual (attracted to the opposite sex) and homosexual (attracted to the same sex)
11 **radicals** people with extreme views
12 **weirdos** strange people (slang)
13 **patronizing** behaving as if they were better than other people
14 **in the long run** ultimately

15 **with all my heart** completely and sincerely (idiom)
16 **crass** insensitive and offensive
17 **humility** modesty, not thinking oneself better than others
18 **the family of man** the shared experience of being human
19 **Mary Ann** one of the main characters in *Tales of the City*, a close friend of the narrator's

FIRST READING

A Thinking About the Story

Discuss the following question with a partner.

> Do you think that writing a letter is a more effective way to raise a difficult subject than having a direct conversation? Explain your answer.

B Understanding the Plot

Be prepared to answer the following questions with a partner or your class.

1. Where does Michael live? Give his full address.
2. Why did Michael's previous attempts to write a letter to his parents not succeed?
3. What caused Michael to come out (reveal he is gay) to his mother?
4. How does Michael view Anita Bryant and the Save the Children movement?
5. How does Michael think his mother will feel when she reads the letter? What makes him understand her reaction?
6. How long has Michael known that he is gay?
7. In lines 21–22, Michael predicts that his mother will blame someone for his homosexuality. Who is it? Does Michael agree?
8. What does Michael wish he'd had when he was younger?
9. In which city can we assume Michael grew up?
10. What is the attitude toward gays in the city where Michael currently lives?
11. In lines 40–42, Michael again predicts that his mother will blame someone for his homosexuality. Who is it this time?
12. In what way does sending the letter make Michael feel better?

PART 2

CRITICAL THINKING

A Exploring Themes

Reread "Letter to Mama." Then answer the following questions, which explore the story more deeply.

1. Michael divides his life into two parts: before and after he moved to a new city. Contrast these two parts of his life in as many ways as possible.
2. What kind of relationship does Michael have with his parents?

3. How does Michael view the critics of homosexuality? Support your answer with details from the story.

4. In lines 18–20, Michael uses a simile (a comparison with *like* or *as*) to help convey what it means to be gay. Explain the two parts of the comparison. What does he want his mother to understand?

B Analyzing Style

TONE

Tone reflects the attitude of the author, the narrator, or a particular character toward what's happening in the story. For example, the tone of a story can be formal or informal, optimistic or pessimistic, ironic, sarcastic, regretful, angry, scientific, or loving. It can also change from one point in a story to another. Interpreting the tone correctly is an important part of appreciating a story. If we misread the tone, we may completely lose the message that the author is trying to convey.

In "Letter to Mama," Michael's tone is often informal, using language such as *That would be O.K. . . .* (line 4) and *I wouldn't have written, I guess, . . .* (line 10). Since these expressions are normally used in conversation, they make his letter sound more personal.

Exercise

Answer the following questions.

1. How would you describe the dominant tone in "Letter to Mama"? Give at least two words to describe this tone. Explain your answer.

2. At one point in the second paragraph, Michael's tone changes. How would you describe the change?

3. How do you think Michael's tone will influence the way his mother reacts to the letter?

4. If Anita Bryant had the chance to respond to Michael's letter, what do you think she would say? What tone do you think she would take?

C Judging for Yourself

Express yourself as personally as you like in your answers to the following questions.

1. Why do you think Michael wrote just to his mother rather than to both his parents?

2. In your view, was Michael right to send his letter, or should he have remained silent? Explain your answer.

3. What are some of the possible ways that Michael's parents might react to his letter? Which do you think is most likely? Explain your answer.

D Making Connections

Answer the following questions in a small group.

1. In your culture, what are some subjects that people have a hard time discussing with their parents?
2. How is homosexuality regarded in your country or culture?
3. In your country, are some cities or regions more progressive and others more conservative? What are some of the main subjects that people have different views about?

E Debate

Decide whether you are for or against the following statement. Write several arguments that support your view. Share your points with a classmate who has taken the opposite position.

Parents should love their children unconditionally.

PART 3 **GRAMMAR IN CONTEXT**

SUFFIXES

A **suffix** consists of one or more letters that come at the end of a word. Suffixes have a grammatical function: they indicate that a word is a noun, a verb, an adjective, or an adverb. Some suffixes also add a particular meaning. For example, –*less* is an adjective suffix that means *without*. Therefore, *limitless* (line 54) is an adjective that means *without limit*. By learning common suffixes, you will often be able to figure out the meaning of a new word without using a dictionary.

1. Noun suffixes

The following suffixes indicate the state or quality of something: –*ance/–ence*, –*dom*, –*hood*, –*ty/–ity*, –*ment*, –*ness*, –*ship*, –*sion/–tion*.

> toler**ance** (line 53), *wis**dom**, child**hood**, responsibil**ity*** (line 13), *govern**ment**, kind**ness*** (line 55), *friend**ship**, rejec**tion*** (line 18)

The following suffixes indicate a person who is practicing a profession or performing an action: –*er*, –*or*, –*ist*.

> teach**er** (line 25), *speak**er**, doct**or*** (line 25), *psycholog**ist***

2. Verb suffixes

The following suffixes indicate making or becoming something: –*ate*, –*ify*, –*ize*, –*en*.

> oper**ate**, *just**ify**, real**ize*** (line 3), *hard**en***

---

3. Adjective suffixes

The following suffixes indicate being full of something or being related to something: *–al, –ant, –ful, –ic, –ious/–ous, –ish, –y.*

  music**al**, ignor**ant** (line 15), help**ful**, trag**ic**, anx**ious**, self**ish**, sorr**y** (line 16)

The suffix *–able/–ible* indicates that something is possible.

  memor**able**, respons**ible** (line 44)

The suffix *–less* means *without*.

  limit**less** (line 54), child**less**

4. Adverb suffixes

The suffix *–ly / –ily* can only be attached to an adjective. It turns the adjective into an adverb.

  conscious**ly** (line 61), successful**ly**, happ**ily**

Sometimes words contain more than one suffix. The final suffix determines the part of speech. For example, the adjective *intentional* combines *–tion* and *–al*, and the adverb *helpfully* combines *–ful* and *–ly*.

Exercise 1

Underline the suffix in each of the following words. Write the part of speech on the line.

1. foolish (line 6) _____

2. especially (line 8) _____

3. involvement (line 11) _____

4. basic (line 19) _____

5. mentor (line 22) _____

6. sexuality (line 33) _____

7. banker (line 36) _____

8. patronize (line 38) _____

9. passion (line 55) _____

10. sensitivity (line 55) _____

Exercise 2

Look at the following words from the story. Use suffixes to form new words as indicated. The first one is done for you as an example.

1. cruel (line 15)   [noun]   *cruelty* _____
2. fear (line 18)   [adjective]   _____
3. nature (line 19)   [adverb]   _____
4. sick (line 26)   [noun]   _____
5. peace (line 26)   [adverb]   _____
6. judge (line 51)   [noun]   _____
7. neighbor (line 51)   [noun]   _____
8. strength (line 56)   [verb]   _____
9. consciously (line 61)   [noun]   _____
10. value (line 64)   [adjective]   _____

Exercise 3

With a partner, complete the following chart with correct forms of the words. First do the exercise without using a dictionary. Then check your answers. The first row is done for you as an example.

NOUN	VERB	ADJECTIVE	ADVERB
creation	create	*creative*	*creatively*
_____	_____	_____	helplessly
_____	hope	_____	_____
softness	_____	_____	_____
sympathy	_____	_____	_____
_____	direct	_____	_____
_____	_____	sleepy	_____
		wide	

Exercise 4

Complete the following sentences with the correct choice in parentheses. Use the suffixes to help you make the right choice.

1. You are too old for this _____! Start acting like a grownup. (fool, foolishness, foolish)

2. Both countries say they want peace, but I am not _____ about it. (hope, hopeful, hopefully)

3. I want to do something about my _____ of world history. (ignorant, ignorance, ignore)

4. This is a really complicated plan. Can we _____ it at all? (simple, simply, simplify)

5. Most research shows that _____ foods are better for your health than artificial ones. (nature, natural, naturalize)

6. My grandmother's diamond ring is my most _____ possession. (value, valuably, valuable)

7. If you want these pants to fit well, I will need to know the correct _____ for your waist. (measure, measurement, measurable)

8. I don't think my _____ responsibilities include doing your laundry! (parental, parent, parenthood)

9. Do you think that computers will ever have _____? (conscious, consciously, consciousness)

10. Even if you don't agree with her, you should listen _____ to your girlfriend's concerns. (sensitively, sensitivity, sensitive)

PART 4 VOCABULARY BUILDING

IDIOMS WITH *HEART*

English has many **idioms** involving body parts. For example, *keep a cool head* means *stay calm*, and *give someone a leg up* means *help someone*. In particular, there are quite a few idioms that include the word *heart*. For example, in the story, Michael says, "If you and Papa are responsible for the way I am, then I thank you *with all my heart*"(lines 44–45). The idiom *with all my heart* means *completely and sincerely*, so Michael is saying that he is deeply grateful.

Exercise 1

With a partner, match each of the following idioms to its definition.
If necessary, use a dictionary to help you.

_____ 1. follow your heart

_____ 2. have a change of heart

_____ 3. have a heart of gold

_____ 4. learn something by heart

_____ 5. break someone's heart

_____ 6. lose heart

_____ 7. take something to heart

_____ 8. a heart-to-heart

a. make someone very unhappy and disappointed

b. memorize

c. stop being hopeful

d. consider something seriously and learn from it

e. be unusually kind and generous

f. an honest and personal conversation

g. reverse a decision

h. do what you are passionate about

Exercise 2

Complete the following sentences with the appropriate idiom from the left-hand column in Exercise 1. You may need to change the form slightly.

1. If my girlfriend doesn't agree to marry me, it will

   _____.

2. You need to have _____ with your daughter about her recent behavior.

3. When I was deciding whether to study law or music, my professor advised me to _____.

4. Your father was right when he told you to focus on your education. You should _____ his words

   _____.

5. The professor _____ and gave her students more time on their exam.

6. My mother encourages me never to

   _____ when life gets difficult.

7. I hear that my neighbor paid for the education of a boy who couldn't afford college. She must _____.

8. Our poetry teacher believed that we should _____ our favorite poems _____.

WORDS EXPRESSING ATTITUDES

When Michael talks about the people of San Francisco, he says, "Their attitude is neither patronizing nor pitying." His letter is filled with words that refer to attitudes, which are the ways that people think and feel. Some of these words are positive, and others are negative.

Exercise 3

The adjectives in the left-hand column refer to attitudes. With a partner, match each adjective to the most closely connected action in the right-hand column. Then discuss which adjectives are positive and which are negative.

_____	1. foolish	a.	listen carefully to an opposing point of view
_____	2. cruel	b.	devote yourself to a cause
_____	3. ignorant	c.	hurt a pet
_____	4. fearful	d.	stay out late before an exam
_____	5. ashamed	e.	notice how someone is feeling
_____	6. tolerant	f.	refuse to read about a subject
_____	7. passionate	g.	run away from a strange noise
_____	8. sensitive	h.	make an embarrassing mistake

Exercise 4

Work with a partner. Each of you should choose two of the following questions. Take turns explaining your answers.

1. Think of a time when you felt particularly foolish. What was the situation?

2. What is a cruel activity that you wish you could prevent?

3. What do you feel most passionate about?

4. What sorts of jobs do you think are best done by people who are sensitive?

5. Is there anything in your country's history that some of its citizens feel ashamed about? Do you agree or disagree with this feeling?

6. Is there a subject you're ignorant about that you would like to understand better?

7. Are there any problems in the world that make you fearful about the future?

8. Is there anything you've become more tolerant about over time?

PART 5

WRITING ACTIVITIES

1. Write a letter to your parents in which you discuss a difficult topic. Explain the issue and say why you've found it hard to talk to them directly. Conclude your answer with a sentence or two about how you feel after expressing your thoughts in writing.

2. Have you ever lied about something important? Write a paragraph in which you describe the deception and the reasons for it. Then write a paragraph in which you explain whether you think you made the right choice.

3. The award-winning movie *Beginners* (2010) is based on a true story about a father who comes out as gay at the age of seventy-five, six months after his wife's death. As the father adopts an openly gay life, his son struggles to accept the change. In recent years, films from around the world have explored the experience of being gay or lesbian from many different angles. Write a short review of a movie that examines this subject. Outline the plot, describe the major themes, and say how you feel about the way the issues are portrayed.

14 ∼ The Last Word Was Love

William Saroyan
(1908–1981)

William Saroyan was born in California to Armenian immigrants. He was three years old when his father died, and the family struggled financially. At age fifteen Saroyan left school and became a writer. Many of his stories were inspired by his rural childhood and by his family's immigrant experiences. In 1934 Saroyan achieved fame with his collection *The Daring Young Man on the Flying Trapeze*. Its stories dealt with the hard times of the Great Depression in a warm and humorous way. Saroyan's best-known collection, *My Name Is Aram* (1940), became an international best seller. His play *The Time of Your Life* (1939) won the Pulitzer Prize, and his script for the movie *The Human Comedy* (1943) won an Oscar for best story. His last book, *Obituaries* (1979), was nominated for a National Book Award.

The Last Word Was Love

A difficult year tests a family's bonds.

A long time ago when I was eleven my mother and my father had a prolonged quarrel.[1]

The quarrel picked up[2] the minute my father got home from work at Graff's, where he was a forty-seven-year-old
5 assistant—to everybody. Graff's sold everything from food to ready-made clothing, animal traps, and farm implements.[3] My father had taken the job only for the daily wage of three dollars, which he received in coin[4] at the end of every twelve-hour day. He didn't mind the nature of the work, even though his profession
10 was teaching, and he didn't care that it might end at any moment, without notice.[5]

He'd already had the job six months, from late summer to early spring, when the quarrel began to get on my brother's nerves.[6] I didn't even begin to *notice* the quarrel until Ralph pointed it out to
15 me. I admired him so much that I joined him in finding fault with[7] my mother and father.

First, though, I'd better describe the quarrel, if that's possible.

To begin with, there was my mother running the house,[8] and there was my father working at Graff's. There was my brother,
20 Ralph, at the top of his class at high school. There I was near the bottom of my class at junior high. And there was our nine-year-old sister, Rose, just enjoying life without any fuss.

All I can say about my mother is that she was a woman—to me a very beautiful one. She had a way of moving very quickly from a
25 singing-and-laughing gladness to a silent-and-dark discontent[9] that bothered my father. I remember hearing him say to her again and again, "Ann, what *is* it?"

Alas,[10] the question was always useless, making my mother cry and my father leave the house.

---

1 **prolonged quarrel** argument extending over
a long period of time
2 **picked up** started again
3 **implements** tools
4 **in coin** in cash
5 **without notice** suddenly, without any warning
6 **get on my brother's nerves** annoy my brother
(idiom)

7 **finding fault with** criticizing
8 **running the house** managing everything
at home
9 **discontent** desire for something more in life
10 **alas** unfortunately (literary expression)

30 During the long quarrel my father seemed hopelessly perplexed and outwitted[11] by something unexpected and unwelcome, which he was determined nevertheless to control and banish.[12]

My brother, Ralph, graduated from high school and took a summertime job in a vineyard.[13] He rode eleven miles to the
35 vineyard on his bicycle every morning soon after daybreak and back again a little before dark every evening. His wages were twenty-five cents an hour, and he put in[14] at least ten hours a day. Early in September he had saved a little more than a hundred dollars.

Early one morning he woke me up.
40 "I want to say good-bye now," he said. "I'm going to San Francisco."

"What for?"

"I can't stay here any more."

Except for the tears in his eyes, I believe I would have said,
45 "Well, good luck, Ralph," but the tears made that impossible. He was as big as my father. The suit he was wearing was my father's, which my mother had altered for him. *What were the tears for?* Would I have them in my own eyes in a moment, too, after all the years of imitating him to *never* have them, and having succeeded except for
50 the two or three times I had let them go when I had been alone, and nobody knew? If the tears came into my eyes, too, what would they be for? Everything I knew I'd learned from my brother, not from school, and everything he knew he'd learned from my father. So now what did we know? What did my father know? What did my
55 brother? What did I?

I got out of bed and jumped into my clothes and went outside to the backyard. Under the old sycamore tree was the almost completed raft[15] my brother and I had been making in our spare time, to launch[16] one day soon on Kings River.
60 "I'll finish it alone," I thought. "I'll float down Kings River alone."

My brother came out of the house quietly, holding an old straw suitcase.

"I'll finish the raft," I said. I believed my brother would say something in the same casual[17] tone of voice, and then turn and
65 walk away, and that would be that.[18]

---

11 **perplexed and outwitted** confused and defeated
12 **banish** get rid of
13 **vineyard** farm where grapes are grown for wine
14 **put in** worked

15 **raft** flat wooden boat
16 **launch** put a boat in water for the first time
17 **casual** not too serious
18 **that would be that** that would be the end of the conversation (informal)

Instead, though, he set the suitcase down and came to the raft. He stepped onto it and sat down, as if we'd just launched the raft and were sailing down Kings River. He put his hand over the side, as if into the cold water of Kings River, and he looked around, as

70 if the raft were passing between vineyards and orchards.[19] After a moment he got up, stepped out of the raft, and picked up the suitcase. There were no tears in his eyes now, but he just couldn't say goodbye. For a moment I thought he was going to give up the idea of leaving home and go back to bed. Instead, he said, "I'll never

75 go into that house again."

"Do you hate them? Is that why?"

"No," he said, but now he began to cry, as if he were eight or nine years old, not almost seventeen.

I picked up the raft, tipped it over,[20] and jumped on it until some

80 of the boards we had so carefully nailed together broke. Then I began to run. I didn't turn around to look at him again.

I ran and walked all the way to where we had planned to launch the raft, about six miles. I sat on the riverbank and tried to think.

It didn't do any good, though. I just didn't understand, that's all.

85 When I got home it was after eleven in the morning. I was very hungry, and I wanted to sit down and eat. My father was at his job at Graff's. My sister was out of the house, and my mother didn't seem to want to look at me. She put food on the table—more than usual, so I was pretty sure she knew something, or at any rate

90 suspected.

At last she said, "Who smashed[21] the raft?"

"I did."

"Why?"

"I got mad at my brother."

95 "Why?"

"I just got mad."

"Eat your food."

She went into the living room, and I ate my food. When I went into the living room she was working at the sewing machine with

100 another of my father's suits.

"This one's for you," she said.

"When can I wear it?"

"Next Sunday. It's one of your father's oldest, when he was slimmer. It'll be a good fit. Do you like it?"

---

19 **orchards** land covered in fruit trees
20 **tipped it over** pushed it onto its side

21 **smashed** broke into pieces

105 "Yes."

She put the work aside[22] and tried to smile, and then *did*, a little.

"She doesn't know what's happened," I thought. And then I thought, "Maybe she *does*, and this is the way she is."

"Your brother's bike is in the garage," she said. "Where's *he*?"

110 "On his way to San Francisco."

"Where have you been?"

"I took a walk."

"A *long* walk?"

"Yes."

115 "Why?"

"I wanted to be alone."

My mother waited a moment and then she said, "Why is your brother on his way to San Francisco?"

"Because—" But I just couldn't tell her.

120 "It's all right," she said. "Tell me."

"Because you and Pop[23] fight so much."

"*Fight?*"

"Yes."

"*Do we?*" my mother said.

125 "I don't know. Are you going to make him come home? Is Pop going to go and get him?"

"No."

"Does he *know*?"

"Yes. He told me."

130 "When?"

"Right after you ran off, and your brother began to walk to the depot.[24] Your father saw the whole thing."

"Didn't he want to stop him?"

"No. Now, go out and repair the raft."

135 I worked hard every day and finished the raft in two weeks. One evening my father helped me get it onto a truck he'd hired.[25] We drove to Kings River, launched it, and sailed down the river about twelve miles. My father brought a letter out of his pocket and read it out loud. It was addressed to Dear Mother and Father. All it said

140 was that Ralph had found a job that he liked, and was going to go to college when the fall semester began, and was well and happy. The last word of the letter was love.

---

22 **she put the work aside** she stopped working for a short time
23 **Pop** Father (old-fashioned)
24 **depot** train or bus station
25 **hired** rented

My father handed me the letter and I read the word for myself.

That Christmas my father sent me to San Francisco to spend a
145 few days with my brother. It was a great adventure for me, because
my brother was so different now—almost like my father, except
that he lived in a furnished room,[26] not in a house full of people. He
wanted to know about the raft, so I told him I'd sailed it and had
put it away for the winter.

150   "You come down next summer and we'll sail it together, the way
we'd planned," I said.

    "No," he said. "We've *already* sailed it together. It's all yours now."

My own son is sixteen years old now, and has made me aware
lately that his mother and I have been quarreling for some time.
155 Nothing new, of course—the same general quarrel—but neither his
mother nor I had ever before noticed that it annoyed him. Later on
this year, or perhaps next year, I know he's going to have a talk with
his younger brother, and then take off.[27] I want to be ready when
that happens, so I can keep his mother from trying to stop him. He's
160 a good boy, and I don't mind at all that he thinks I've made a mess
of my life,[28] which is one thing he is *not* going to do.

    Of course he isn't.

---

26 **furnished room** rented bedroom that
comes with furniture
27 **take off** leave

28 **made a mess of my life** ruined my life

FIRST READING

A Thinking About the Story

Discuss the following question with a partner.

> In your view, was the narrator's family a loving family? Explain your
> answer.

B Understanding the Plot

Be prepared to answer the following questions with a partner or your class.

1. How old is each of the three children at the start of the story?
2. What job does the narrator's father have? What did he do before?

3. When does the narrator notice his parents' quarrel? Why does he care about it? (lines 14–16)

4. What does the narrator's mother do during the day?

5. Is the narrator a good student? What about his brother?

6. How would you describe the moods of the narrator's mother? Answer in your own words. (lines 23–29)

7. What does Ralph do over the summer? Why does he save up his money?

8. Do the brothers sail down the river together on their raft? Explain your answer.

9. At first, how does the narrator act when he learns what Ralph is planning to do? (lines 56–65)

10. What causes the narrator to start responding more emotionally to Ralph's decision? What action does the narrator take?

11. How does the narrator's mother know what happened?

12. What information does Ralph give his parents in his letter?

13. When the narrator visits San Francisco, how does Ralph seem to have changed? (lines 144–149)

14. What do we learn about the narrator's relationship with his own wife and son?

PART 2

CRITICAL THINKING

A Exploring Themes

Reread "The Last Word Was Love." Then answer the following questions, which explore the story more deeply.

1. How would you describe the personality of the narrator's father? Give examples from the story. Are the two sons similar to their father? Explain your answer.

2. In lines 44–55, what do we learn about how the narrator views his older brother?

3. What do the two suits the mother alters for the brothers represent in the story?

4. What does Ralph's letter reveal about how he views family ties? Consider the story's title in your answer.

5. What does the story suggest about the relationship between one generation and the next?

B Analyzing Style

INFERENCE

Writers must always choose what to say explicitly and what to suggest. Much of the important information in a story is often not stated directly. Instead, we need to use **inference** to figure it out from what we're given.

The narrator in "The Last Word Was Love" is looking back on his childhood. He tells the story mostly from the perspective of his eleven-year-old self. Because the narrator is only a boy, he gives us a surface view of his family life. We often have to take the extra step of inferring the significance of his statements. For example, the narrator mentions that his mother alters two of his father's suits for Ralph and himself. Although he doesn't say it explicitly, this suggests that the family cannot afford to buy new suits.

Exercise 1

Answer the following questions.

1. What do you think the parents' *prolonged quarrel* (line 2) was about? Explain your answer.
2. What might we infer from the fact that the father works as a shop assistant and not in his profession as a teacher?
3. Does the family live in an urban or a rural setting? How do we know?
4. What is suggested about Ralph's character in lines 33–38?
5. Why do you think Ralph's father doesn't try to stop him from leaving home? Explain your answer.
6. At the end of the story, the narrator says that his son won't make a mess of his life. Do you think the narrator really believes this? Explain your answer.

SYMBOL

A **symbol** is one thing that stands for another. Often a symbol is something concrete (such as an object or a place) that represents something abstract (such as an emotion or an idea).

Some symbols are general, which means that their association is widely understood. For example, the shape of a heart symbolizes love. Other symbols stand for something only within a particular work of literature. In "The Last Word Was Love," the raft is an important and complex symbol.

Exercise 2

Answer the following questions.

1. In lines 66–73, Ralph pretends to sail the raft down the river. List the details of the trip. What does this imaginary trip on the raft represent for Ralph? How do you think Ralph is feeling?

2. What might the breaking of the raft symbolize?

3. After the raft is broken, it seems to become a symbol of unity. How does the raft unite the family? In your answer, consider how the two brothers, their mother, and their father all play a role in getting the raft ready.

4. What might Ralph mean when he says to the narrator, "We've *already* sailed it together. It's all yours now"? (line 152)

5. Where does the narrator go on the raft after he finishes repairing it? What might the trip symbolize?

C Judging for Yourself

Express yourself as personally as you like in your answers to the following questions.

1. Do you think that Ralph had a successful career? Why or why not?

2. In your opinion, should Ralph's parents have tried to stop him from leaving home?

3. The two brothers are different in many ways. Do you think their differences come from their positions in the family (older and younger brother) or from the personalities they were born with?

D Making Connections

Answer the following questions in a small group.

1. In your country, is it common for young people to leave home right after high school?

2. Do the majority of women work or stay at home in your country? Explain your answer.

3. How do high school students tend to spend their summer vacation in your country?

4. Are there particular cities in your country that attract young people? Explain why they are appealing.

E Debate

Decide whether you are for or against the following statement. Write several arguments that support your view. Share your points with a classmate who has taken the opposite position.

Children tend to repeat the mistakes of their parents.

PART 3

GRAMMAR IN CONTEXT

COUNT AND NONCOUNT NOUNS

Nouns can be divided into two categories: **count** and **noncount**. Count nouns can be singular or plural. Noncount nouns can only be singular. For example, *clothing* (line 6) is a noncount noun and cannot be plural; however, *suit* (line 46) is a count noun with the plural form *suits*.

1. A **count noun** is a noun that can be counted. This means that when thinking about a count noun, you can ask the question *how many?*

   * A count noun can be plural.

     *He looked around, as if the raft were passing between **vineyards and orchards.*** (lines 69–70)

   * A count noun can have a number before it.

     *I worked hard every day and finished the raft in two **weeks.*** (line 135)

   * The indefinite article *a/an* can precede a singular count noun.

     *After a **moment** he got up.* (lines 70–71)

     Note: For practice with definite and indefinite articles, see pages 205–208.

2. A **noncount** noun is a noun that cannot be counted.

   * Noncount nouns cannot be plural. Since a noncount noun is singular, the verb that follows it must be singular as well.

     Incorrect: *These informations are valuable.*

     Correct: *This **information** is valuable.*

   * It is not possible to use a number or the indefinite article *a/an* with a noncount noun.

     Incorrect: *Ralph spent hours after school on three homeworks.*

     Incorrect: *Ralph spent hours after school on a homework.*

     Correct: *Ralph spent hours after school on **homework.***

- Many noncount nouns are abstract. Professions, feelings, and academic subjects are typically noncount.

    *He didn't mind the nature of the work, even though his profession was **teaching**.* (lines 8–10)

    *She had a way of moving very quickly from **happiness** to **sadness**.* (adapted from lines 24–25)

    *Ralph decided to study **chemistry**.*

- Some noncount nouns refer to a category. However, the individual parts of the category may be count nouns.

    *Ralph worked hard all summer and saved his **money**.* [noncount]

    *Early in September he had saved a little more than a hundred **dollars**.* (lines 37–38) [count]

- Nouns referring to liquids are usually noncount. These include *water, milk, tea, coffee,* and *gasoline*. Many nouns referring to foods are noncount as well. These include *bread, fish, meat, sugar,* and *rice*.

    *I drink **coffee** when I get up each morning.*

3. Some nouns can be count or noncount depending on their meaning or use. These include *wine, college, experience, death, room,* and *time*.

    *I had not cried except for the two or three **times** when I had been alone.* (adapted from lines 48–51) [count]

    *My brother and I made a raft in our spare **time**.* (adapted from lines 57–59) [noncount]

    *. . . he lived in a furnished **room** . . .* (line 147) [count]

    *The raft has **room** for two people.* [noncount]

Exercise 1

The following sentences come from the story or are adapted from the story. Say whether each underlined noun is count or noncount.

1. The <u>quarrel</u> picked up the minute my father got home from <u>work</u> at Graff's . . . (lines 3–4)

2. Graff's sold everything from <u>clothing</u> to <u>farm implements</u>. (adapted from lines 5–6)

3. There was our <u>sister</u> Rose, just enjoying <u>life</u> without any fuss. (adapted from lines 21–22)

4. Ralph took a job in a <u>vineyard</u>. (adapted from lines 33–34)

5. His wages were twenty-five <u>cents</u> an hour . . . (lines 36–37)

6. My brother came out of the house quietly, holding an old straw <u>suitcase</u>. (lines 61–62)

7. He put his hand over the side, as if into the cold <u>water</u> of Kings River . . . (lines 68–69)

8. I sat on the <u>riverbank</u> and tried to think. (line 83)

9. She put <u>food</u> on the table . . . (line 88)

10. Ralph had found a <u>job</u> that he liked, and was going to go to <u>college</u> when the fall semester began. (adapted from lines 140–141)

Exercise 2

Complete the following sentences with the correct choice in parentheses.

1. It is hard to find good farming _____. (equipment/ equipments)

2. Mathematics _____ good training for many professions. (is/are)

3. A thousand _____ is a lot of money. (dollar/dollars)

4. The queen's jewelry _____ in the sunlight. (shine/ shines)

5. Does your bedroom have enough _____ for your furniture? (space/spaces)

6. Do you think your _____ will be hard tonight? (homework/homeworks)

7. Wearing the right _____ to an interview may help you get a job. (clothing/clothings)

8. I will be studying in Brazil for three _____ this summer. (month/months)

9. The economics lecture was full of useful _____. (information/informations)

10. I always try to remember _____ wisdom of my grandmother. (a/the)

QUANTIFIERS

Quantifiers answer the questions *how many?* and *how much?* To use the correct quantifier, you need to be aware of whether your nouns are count or noncount.

- The quantifiers *some, any,* and *enough* modify both count and noncount nouns.

    We carefully nailed **some** boards together to make a raft. [count]
    At first, Ralph had **some** trouble getting used to city life. [noncount]

    The parents didn't want to listen to **any** complaints from their children. [count]
    My father never expressed **any** sadness about his job in a store. [noncount]

    The narrator felt he had shed **enough** tears, so he dried his eyes. [count]
    Ralph saved **enough** money to leave home. [noncount]

- The quantifiers *many* and *few* modify only count nouns.

    The brothers heard **many** quarrels between their parents.

    Very **few** children like to hear their parents argue.

- The quantifiers *much* and *little* modify only noncount nouns.

    How **much** wood did the brothers use to build their raft?

    The narrator had very **little** time to prepare himself for Ralph's departure.

Exercise 3

Complete each of the following sentences with the correct quantifier in parentheses.

1. They now have _____ information to make up their minds. (enough/few)

2. We have told you _____ times not to do that. (many/much)

3. I deserve very _____ credit for her success. (few/little)

4. It doesn't take _____ time to complete this task. (many/much)

5. I don't know whether we have _____ students in the class. (enough/much)

6. I made _____ changes to my speech at the last minute. (much/some)

7. There will be very _____ opportunities to see this exhibition. (few/little)

8. Do _____ friends of yours live in Asia? (much/any)

9. Our sister never puts _____ butter on her bread.
   (any/many)

10. I don't have _____ experience with fixing cars.
    (many/much)

PART 4

VOCABULARY BUILDING

PHRASAL VERBS WITH MORE THAN ONE MEANING

A **phrasal verb** consists of a base verb plus one or more particles. The particles can be adverbs or prepositions. Phrasal verbs are idiomatic, so it is often difficult to figure out the meaning of a phrasal verb by looking at its separate parts.

Many phrasal verbs have more than one meaning. For example, the phrasal verb *run off* can be used in several entirely different ways.

> *Right after you **ran off**, your brother walked to the depot.* (adapted from lines 131–132)
> Here, *run off* means *leave suddenly.*

> *Please **run off** ten more copies of this handout.*
> Here, *run off* means *print copies on a copy machine.*

Exercise 1

In each of the following pairs of sentences, the first sentence contains a phrasal verb from the story. The second sentence contains the same phrasal verb used in a different way. With a partner, explain the two meanings of each phrasal verb.

1. The quarrel *picked up* the minute my father got home . . . (lines 3–4)
   I *picked up* my daughter from school and took her to her piano lesson.

2. . . . he *put in* at least ten hours a day. (line 37)
   Please *put in* a good word for me with your boss. I'd love to work at your company.

3. She *put* the work *aside* and tried to smile . . . (line 106)
   The parents *put* money *aside* each month in order to pay for their children's college.

4. I told him I'd sailed the raft and had *put it away* for the winter. (adapted from lines 148–149)
   The thief was sentenced to be *put away* for two years for breaking into a house.

5. . . . he's going to have a talk with his younger brother and then *take off*. (lines 157–158)
   Please *take off* your shoes before coming inside.

Exercise 2

Imagine what happens when the narrator visits Ralph in San Francisco. With a partner, write a short conversation between the brothers. Use each phrasal verb from Exercise 1 in at least one of the two ways.

EXPRESSIONS WITH *TIME*

Many expressions in English involve the word *time*. In "The Last Word Was Love," the narrator starts his story with the traditional introduction *a long time ago*. He talks about building a raft with his brother in their *spare time* (lines 58–59), and at the end of the story he comments that he has been quarreling with his wife *for some time* (line 154).

Exercise 3

With a partner, match each expression in the left-hand column with its definition.

_____	**1.** run out of time	**a.** spend time in jail
_____	**2.** for the time being	**b.** leisure time
_____	**3.** from time to time	**c.** punctually
_____	**4.** lose track of time	**d.** not hurry
_____	**5.** kill time	**e.** not be aware of the time
_____	**6.** on time	**f.** early
_____	**7.** serve time	**g.** occasionally
_____	**8.** spare time	**h.** have no time left
_____	**9.** take (one's) time	**i.** temporarily
_____	**10.** ahead of time	**j.** do something unimportant while waiting

Exercise 4

Complete the following sentences with an appropriate expression from the left-hand column in Exercise 3. You may need to change the form of the verb.

1. I wish I could go to the concert with you, but I'm so busy at work these days that I don't have any _____.

2. If our flight doesn't arrive _____, we might miss our connection.

3. When my friend is working on a difficult mathematics problem, she always _____ and forgets to eat dinner.

4. My doctor's appointment is in half an hour, so I'll _____ in a café.

5. _____. It's more important for you to do this well than to do it quickly.

6. If you take too long on the first half of your exam, you might _____.

7. When you work at a computer all day, it's good to take a break _____.

8. If he hadn't told me about his past, I would never have guessed that my neighbor had _____.

9. You can stay with me _____, but you'll need to find your own place to live soon.

10. There was much less traffic than expected, so we got to the restaurant _____ and had to wait for our friends to arrive.

Exercise 5

Do you know any other expressions with the word *time*? Share them with a partner.

PART 5

WRITING ACTIVITIES

1. The narrator in "The Last Word Was Love" says that he learned everything from his brother. Have you ever had a role model (someone you admired and tried to be like)? It could be someone important in your own life, a person from history, or a character in a movie or book. Write three paragraphs about this role model. In the first paragraph, describe the person. In the second paragraph, say why he or she made such a strong impression on you. In the third paragraph, explain how this role model affected your life.

2. Imagine a conversation between the grown-up narrator and his sixteen-year-old son. Write a dialogue between them that reflects what is going on in the family. Pay attention to the correct use of count and noncount nouns in your writing.

3. *Adventures of Huckleberry Finn* by Mark Twain is a classic American novel about two people who sail down the Mississippi River on a raft. Huck Finn comes from a poor family and runs away in search of freedom and adventure. His companion, Jim, is a black slave who is escaping from slavery. As a result of their travels, Huck grows up and learns from Jim's sense of morality. By the end of the book, Huck is more open-minded and mature than when he began. Write a review of a film or book about a journey that transforms the main character. Outline the plot, explain what kind of journey is taken, and say what the character learns.

15 Girl

Jamaica Kincaid
(b. 1949)

Jamaica Kincaid was born on the Caribbean island of Antigua when it was a British colony. At age seventeen she went to work as a nanny in New York. Her short story "Girl" appeared in the *New Yorker* in 1978, and she wrote for that magazine for twenty years. Kincaid's short stories were collected in the anthology *At the Bottom of the River* (1992). She has written a number of novels, including *Annie John* (1986), *Lucy* (1990), and *Mr. Potter* (2002). Her memoir *My Brother* (1997) was written after her brother's death from AIDS. It was nominated for the National Book Award. In her nonfiction book *A Small Place* (1988), Kincaid strongly criticized British rule in Antigua as well as the choices made by the Antiguans after independence. Her writing is both personal and political. It often reflects the difficult relationship she had with her mother as well as the continuing effects of colonization.

Girl

A girl receives advice on how to behave properly.

Wash the white clothes on Monday and put them on the stone heap; wash the color clothes on Tuesday and put them on the clothesline to dry; don't walk barehead in the hot sun; cook pumpkin fritters[1] in very hot sweet oil; soak your
5 little cloths[2] right after you take them off; when buying cotton to make yourself a nice blouse, be sure that it doesn't have gum[3] on it, because that way it won't hold up well[4] after a wash; soak salt fish overnight before you cook it; is it true that you sing benna in Sunday school?[5]; always eat your food in such a way that it won't
10 turn someone else's stomach;[6] on Sundays try to walk like a lady and not like the slut you are so bent on becoming;[7] don't sing benna in Sunday school; you mustn't speak to wharf-rat boys,[8] not even to give directions; don't eat fruits on the street—flies will follow you; *but I don't sing benna on Sundays at all and never in Sunday school;*
15 this is how to sew on a button; this is how to make a button-hole for the button you have just sewed on; this is how to hem a dress[9] when you see the hem coming down and so to prevent yourself from looking like the slut I know you are so bent on becoming; this is how you iron your father's khaki shirt so that it doesn't have a
20 crease; this is how you iron your father's khaki pants so that they don't have a crease; this is how you grow okra[10]—far from the house, because okra tree harbors[11] red ants; when you are growing dasheen,[12] make sure it gets plenty of water or else it makes your throat itch when you are eating it; this is how you sweep a corner; this
25 is how you sweep a whole house; this is how you sweep a yard; this is how you smile to someone you don't like too much; this is how you smile to someone you don't like at all; this is how you smile to someone you like completely; this is how you set a table for tea; this is how you set a table for dinner; this is how you set a table
30 for dinner with an important guest; this is how you set a table for

---

1 **fritters** small pieces of fried food
2 **little cloths** fabric used by women during menstruation
3 **gum** sticky plant substance
4 **it won't hold up well** it won't last long
5 **sing benna in Sunday school** sing Antiguan folk music when learning about Christianity
6 **turn someone else's stomach** make someone else feel sick (idiom)

7 **not like the slut you are so bent on becoming** not like the sexually immoral person you are determined to be
8 **wharf-rat boys** dishonest boys who steal from ships or buildings by the water
9 **hem a dress** sew the bottom of a dress
10 **okra** a vegetable
11 **harbors** shelters
12 **dasheen** a plant with an edible root

lunch; this is how you set a table for breakfast; this is how to behave in the presence of men who don't know you very well, and this way they won't recognize immediately the slut I have warned you against becoming; be sure to wash every day, even if it is with your
35 own spit;[13] don't squat down[14] to play marbles—you are not a boy, you know; don't pick people's flowers—you might catch something; don't throw stones at blackbirds, because it might not be a blackbird at all; this is how to make a bread pudding; this is how to make doukona;[15] this is how to make pepper pot;[16] this is how to make a
40 good medicine for a cold; this is how to make a good medicine to throw away a child before it even becomes a child; this is how to catch a fish; this is how to throw back a fish you don't like, and that way something bad won't fall on you; this is how to bully a man;[17] this is how a man bullies you; this is how to love a man, and if this
45 doesn't work there are other ways, and if they don't work don't feel too bad about giving up; this is how to spit up in the air if you feel like it, and this is how to move quick so that it doesn't fall on you; this is how to make ends meet;[18] always squeeze bread to make sure it's fresh; *but what if the baker won't let me feel the bread?*; you mean to
50 say that after all you are really going to be the kind of woman who the baker won't let near the bread?

---

13 **spit** water from the mouth
14 **squat down** sit on one's heels
15 **doukona** a West Indian dish wrapped in a banana leaf
16 **pepper pot** a spicy West Indian dish

17 **bully a man** manipulate a man into doing what you want him to do
18 **make ends meet** manage to live on very little money (idiom)

PART 1 **FIRST READING**

A Thinking About the Story

Discuss the following question with a partner.

What words would you use to describe the personality of the main speaker? Explain your answer.

B Understanding the Plot

Be prepared to answer the following questions with a partner or your class.

1. Who do you think the main speaker is? Do we know for sure?

2. How old do you think the girl is? Justify your answer.

3. The story consists of advice about how to behave. This advice falls into several categories. For each of the following categories, give at least two examples of the speaker's advice.

    a. housekeeping

    b. cooking

    c. being a moral person

    d. staying healthy and clean

    e. interacting with men

4. The girl interrupts the speaker twice. What does the girl say? How does the speaker react each time?

5. What are the three ways of smiling that the speaker mentions? (lines 25–28) What is she trying to teach the girl in these lines?

6. What kind of *medicine* is the speaker talking about in lines 40–41?

7. Why does the speaker tell the girl to throw unwanted fish back in the water?

8. The speaker says that bakers won't let certain women touch their bread. (lines 49–51) What kind of woman does she mean?

PART 2 CRITICAL THINKING

A Exploring Themes

Reread "Girl." Then answer the following questions, which explore the story more deeply.

1. Why does the speaker give the girl so much advice? What is she particularly concerned about?

2. How does the speaker act toward the girl? How would you describe the way that she presents her advice?

3. From the speaker's point of view, what is the role of women in society?

4. What is the importance of the title? What is the effect of never learning the girl's name?

B Analyzing Style

INFERENCE

"Girl" is composed almost entirely of advice given by one person. As a result, the perspective is limited. This forces us to make frequent use of **inference**, which means coming to conclusions that are suggested but not stated explicitly. For example, we don't see the speaker from the outside, so her personality is never described directly. Instead, we need to infer her personality from her words. Also, since the speaker is talking to someone who is close to her, there are many things that she doesn't need to say. For example, she never says where the story takes place. However, from expressions such as growing *dasheen* and singing *benna*, we can infer that the characters don't live in the United States. By looking up these expressions, we can determine that the characters live in the Caribbean.

Exercise 1

Answer the following questions.

1. What can we infer about the economic situation of the characters? Explain your answer.

2. What can we infer about the reason that the speaker doesn't want the girl to sing *benna* in Sunday school?

3. The speaker suggests that the girl will make a certain impression on the men she meets. (lines 31–34) What is it? Why do you think the speaker is concerned about this?

4. What might we infer about the girl from how little she interrupts the speaker?

PROSE POEM

"Girl" isn't easy to place into a literary category. The story is told in one long paragraph of *prose*, which means it is written in ordinary sentences. However, "Girl" also has a number of features usually associated with poetry. For example, it includes rhythmic language, many types of repetition, and nonstandard punctuation. It also fits many ideas into a small space. Since it contains elements of both prose and poetry, "Girl" may be considered a **prose poem**.

Answer the following questions.

1. The author repeats a variety of words and phrases that give the story a distinct rhythm. What repetitions can you find?
2. The repetitions reveal a lot about the speaker's personality and her concerns. What do we learn from them?
3. What is the effect of telling the story in one long paragraph? What punctuation is used to separate the sentences? Why do you think the author doesn't use periods?
4. Overall, do you think "Girl" feels more like prose or poetry? Explain your answer.

C Judging for Yourself

Express yourself as personally as you like in your answers to the following questions.

1. How do you think it would feel to receive all this advice? Do you think the girl is likely to follow it?
2. Do you think the girl's perspective on the speaker's advice might change when she grows up? Explain your answer.
3. Did you have a strong reaction to any of the speaker's advice? Explain your answer.
4. Do you think the speaker presents her advice well? Are there ways that she could be more effective? Explain your answer.

D Making Connections

Answer the following questions in a small group.

1. In your culture today, what advice do parents give that many children believe is out of date?
2. In your country, are there particular tasks that are considered to be the responsibility of women?
3. In your culture, what kinds of behavior are not considered appropriate for a girl? What about for a boy?
4. Do you have popular national dishes? What are they? Are they served on certain occasions?

E Debate

Decide whether you are for or against the following statement. Write several arguments that support your view. Share your points with a classmate who has taken the opposite position.

Children should obey their parents.

PART 3

GRAMMAR IN CONTEXT

ARTICLES

The **indefinite article** *a/an* and the **definite article** *the* are used with nouns. The correct use of articles can be difficult, especially for students who do not have articles in their native language.

When deciding which article to use with a noun, it is important to know whether the noun is *count* or *noncount*. For more information about count and noncount nouns, see pages 192–194.

It is also important to know whether the noun is *specific* (a particular thing) or *nonspecific* (a generalization).

> *This is how to make a button-hole for **the** button you have just sewed on.*
> (lines 15–16)

Here, *button* is specific. The sentence is about a particular button (the one that's just been sewed on).

> *This is how to sew on **a** button.* (line 15)

Here, *button* is nonspecific. The sentence is a generalization about buttons. It is not about one particular button.

Use the **definite article** *the* in the following cases:

- with a specific count noun in the singular or plural (where the speaker and the listener both know what is being referred to)

  > *Wash **the** white clothes on Monday and put them on **the** stone heap.* (lines 1–2)

- with a specific noncount noun

  > *I don't agree with **the** advice that my mother gave me this morning.*

- with certain geographical areas such as oceans, mountain ranges, and deserts

  > *Last year we sailed across **the** Atlantic Ocean, climbed **the** Alps, flew over **the** Sahara Desert, and visited **the** Middle East.*

- with countries with a plural name

  > *At the moment I live in **the** United States, but I was born in **the** Philippines.*

Use the **indefinite article** *a/an* with a nonspecific count noun in the singular only.

> *This is how you set **a** table for dinner with **an** important guest.* (lines 29–30)

Use **no article** in the following cases:

- with a nonspecific count noun in the plural

  > *Don't throw stones at blackbirds.* (line 37)

  > *Compare: Don't throw stones at **the** blackbirds in the yard.* [particular blackbirds]

- with a noncount noun like *happiness, advice, wood,* or *tea* when it is nonspecific

  > *When buying cotton to make yourself a nice blouse, be sure that it doesn't have gum on it . . .* (lines 5–7)

  > *My mother gives me advice whenever I see her.*

- when referring to sports or languages

  > *I played football as a child, but now I prefer tennis.*

  > *I wish I had studied Chinese and Spanish in high school.*

- when a mountain's name is preceded by the word *Mount*

  > *Which is higher: Mount Fuji or Mount Kilimanjaro?*

- for countries with a singular name

  > *I hope to visit France and South Korea next year.*

- when referring to a city or street

  > *If you come to Tokyo, I'll take you to the best sushi restaurant in the city.*

  > *My parents live on Fillmore Street.*

Exercise 1

Working with a partner, look at the following sentences. Take turns explaining the use or absence of articles for each of the underlined nouns.

1. Cook pumpkin fritters in very hot sweet oil. (line 4)
2. This is how you grow okra—far from the house . . . (lines 21–22)
3. This is how to behave in the presence of men who don't know you very well. (lines 31–32)
4. This is how to bully a man. (line 43)
5. Always squeeze bread to make sure it's fresh. (lines 48–49)

Exercise 2

Complete the following sentences with the correct article. When no article is needed, leave the space blank.

1. Would you like to visit _____ West Indies with me next year?

2. _____ Russian writer Tolstoy often explores the theme of _____ unhappiness.

3. I want to learn how to play _____ basketball.

4. Our parents taught us always to be kind to _____ animals.

5. I don't usually eat _____ fish, but _____ dish you made looks so good that I'm going to try it.

6. May I have _____ banana please? No, not that one, I want _____ biggest banana in _____ bowl.

7. Almost no one gets _____ "A" in _____ law class that I'm taking.

8. Please buy me _____ loaf of bread at _____ bakery next door.

9. Have you found _____ Pacific Ocean on the map? What about _____ Los Angeles?

10. To get to our home from the subway, walk three blocks to _____ Harwood Avenue and turn right. Our house is _____ third one on _____ left side of _____ street. There is _____ large oak tree in _____ front yard.

Exercise 3

Complete each space in the following letter. Use the correct article or leave the space blank. Then write at least four more sentences of your own to finish the letter, paying attention to your articles.

Dear Jennifer,

    Last night we flew to Antigua, which is _____ island in _____ Caribbean. _____ people here are very friendly.

    Today we ate lunch at _____ best market in _____ neighborhood. It was _____ fascinating experience. We had chicken with _____ rice and _____ vegetables. _____ cucumbers in _____ salad were particularly good. We saw someone eating _____ unusual pineapple dessert, so we decided to try _____ same thing.

    In _____ afternoon. . . .

Best wishes,

_____

Exercise 4

With a partner, ask and answer the following questions in full sentences. Apply the rules about articles.

1. What country do you live in?
2. Do you play any sports? Are there any you would like to learn?
3. Which oceans, if any, have you crossed in your travels?
4. What are some of the emotions that you have felt in the past twenty-four hours?
5. What are some of the most popular foods in your country?
6. What languages can you speak?
7. What advice would you give to someone who was planning a trip to your country?
8. How do you get to your home from the nearest bus or subway stop?
9. In your country, what do people tend to drink throughout the day?
10. What animals do you particularly like or dislike?

PART 4

VOCABULARY BUILDING

IDIOMATIC EXPRESSIONS

"Girl" contains a variety of **idiomatic expressions** whose meaning can be hard to figure out. For example, the speaker warns the girl not to *catch something* (line 36). When the verb *catch* refers to getting sick, it is often used in the expression *catch a cold*. Learning these types of expressions will improve your comprehension and make your spoken English sound more natural.

Exercise 1

Look at the following expressions from the story. Use the footnotes or a dictionary to make sure you understand each expression. Complete the paragraph with the appropriate expressions from the list.

hold up (line 7)	set the table (line 28)
turn someone's stomach (line 10)	pick flowers (line 36)
bent on (line 11)	give up (line 46)
make sure (line 23)	make ends meet (line 48)

The mother instructs her daughter in many ways. She wants to

_____ that the girl has all the information

she needs to be a practical and moral person. She tells the girl that to

_____ she needs to watch her expenses

carefully. The girl should not _____ in

someone else's yard, or she might get sick. When she has guests, the girl

should always _____ properly before

they arrive. She should never eat in an unpleasant way that might

_____. The mother worries that her

daughter is _____ behaving badly. She

hopes that her instructions will _____

over the years and help her daughter become a good wife. However, she

tells the girl that it is all right to _____

if something seems impossible to achieve.

Exercise 2

Complete the following instructions for living in the United States with the expressions from Exercise 1.

1. If you want to _____ on a small budget, don't buy coffee at cafés every day.

2. _____ to check the signs on the street before you park your car.

3. When you _____, put the knife on the right and the fork on the left.

4. If you are _____ mastering English, you should speak it with your friends as much as possible.

5. You shouldn't _____ when you're walking in a park.

6. Keep your mouth closed while eating, or you might _____.

7. Smartphones _____ better if you don't drop them all the time!

8. If a class is difficult, study harder and don't _____.

FOOD IDIOMS

"Girl" contains a number of references to foods, such as *bread* (line 51) and *fish* (lines 41–42). **Idioms** involving food are very common in English and come up regularly in conversation and writing. For example, the idiom *break bread* refers to sharing a meal with someone, and the idiom *be a fish out of water* refers to feeling uncomfortable in one's environment.

Exercise 3

The following sentences all include idioms that refer to food or drink. Working with a partner, try to guess the meaning of each idiom from its context. Then check your answers.

1. You shouldn't invest all your money in one business. It's dangerous to *put all your eggs in one basket*.

2. I appreciate the invitation, but I don't think I'll go. Loud dance parties are *not my cup of tea*.

3. This exam is *a piece of cake*. I'll be finished long before the end of class.

4. Many websites are not very reliable. You should *take* what they say *with a grain of salt*.

5. Each year, my university selects the *cream of the crop* for a special award.

6. Even one *bad apple* can make a company much less pleasant to work for.

Exercise 4

Complete the following sentences in your own words. Share your sentences with a partner.

1. When my friend _____, she was really putting all her eggs in one basket.

2. _____ has never been my cup of tea.

3. Don't worry, _____ is a piece of cake.

4. I heard a rumor that _____, but you should take it with a grain of salt.

5. _____ only accepts the cream of the crop.

6. He really seems like a bad apple. Yesterday, _____.

Exercise 5

Translate into English some common food idioms from your native language. Share them with your partner or the class.

PART 5 # WRITING ACTIVITIES

1. Imagine you have a son or a daughter. Write a speech in which you give your child advice on correct behavior. Before you write, think about what tone of voice you want to convey. For example, you might want to sound loving, encouraging, angry, or worried. Pay attention to the correct use of articles in your speech.

2. Look up Antigua in a book or online. Write three paragraphs about what you learn. In the first paragraph you could describe some physical features of the island; in the second paragraph you could give some details about its culture; and in the third paragraph you could outline Antigua's struggle for independence from Britain.

3. "Girl" paints a short but vivid picture of the characters' lives in Antigua. For example, there are references to food, music, animals, religion, and gender roles. Write a report of one to two pages about a book, movie, or work of art that depicts a culture that's very different from your own. Briefly describe the work, giving details about the culture. Say what you found most interesting.

16 ⟨⟩ Ambush

Tim O'Brien

(b. 1946)

The American writer Tim O'Brien was born in Minnesota. After studying political science in college, he served as a soldier in the Vietnam War. He received the Purple Heart, a medal for being wounded in battle. When he completed his military service, O'Brien went to Harvard to study government. Before graduating, he left to work as a journalist at the *Washington Post*. His first book was a memoir called *If I Die in a Combat Zone: Box Me Up and Send Me Home* (1973). Since then, O'Brien has written several more books dealing with the Vietnam War. His novel *Going After Cacciato* (1978) won the National Book Award, and his short-story collection *The Things They Carried* (1990) has become a modern classic. In 2013, O'Brien became the first fiction writer to win the Pritzker Military Library Literature Award for military writing. He teaches creative writing at Texas State University.

Ambush[1]

A father remembers a wartime experience that he had as a young soldier.

When she was nine, my daughter Kathleen asked if I had ever killed anyone. She knew about the war; she knew I'd been a soldier. "You keep writing these war stories," she said, "so I guess you must've killed somebody." It was a difficult

5   moment, but I did what seemed right, which was to say, "Of course not," and then to take her onto my lap and hold her for a while. Someday, I hope, she'll ask again. But here I want to pretend she's a grown-up. I want to tell her exactly what happened, or what I remember happening, and then I want to say to her that as a little

10 girl she was absolutely right. This is why I keep writing war stories:

He was a short, slender[2] young man of about twenty. I was afraid of him—afraid of something—and as he passed me on the trail I threw a grenade[3] that exploded at his feet and killed him.

Or to go back:

15 Shortly after midnight we moved into the ambush site outside My Khe. The whole platoon[4] was there, spread out in the dense brush[5] along the trail, and for five hours nothing at all happened. We were working in two-man teams—one man on guard while the other slept, switching off[6] every two hours—and I remember

20 it was still dark when Kiowa shook me awake for the final watch. The night was foggy and hot. For the first few moments I felt lost, not sure about directions, groping for[7] my helmet and weapon. I reached out and found three grenades and lined them up in front of me; the pins[8] had already been straightened for quick throwing.

25 And then for maybe half an hour I knelt there and waited. Very gradually, in tiny slivers,[9] dawn began to break through the fog, and from my position in the brush I could see ten or fifteen meters up the trail. The mosquitoes were fierce. I remember slapping at them, wondering if I should wake up Kiowa and ask for some repellent,[10]

30 then thinking it was a bad idea, then looking up and seeing the young man come out of the fog. He wore black clothing and rubber

---

1 **ambush** surprise attack
2 **slender** thin
3 **grenade** small bomb thrown by hand
4 **platoon** small military unit
5 **dense brush** area where bushes grow close together

6 **switching off** changing places
7 **groping for** feeling blindly for
8 **the pins** the safety switches on a grenade
9 **in tiny slivers** in small fragments
10 **repellent** substance that keeps insects away

sandals[11] and a gray ammunition[12] belt. His shoulders were slightly stooped, his head cocked to the side[13] as if listening for something. He seemed at ease.[14] He carried his weapon in one hand, muzzle[15] down, moving without any hurry up the center of the trail. There was no sound at all—none that I can remember. In a way, it seemed, he was part of the morning fog, or my own imagination, but there was also the reality of what was happening in my stomach. I had already pulled the pin on a grenade. I had come up to a crouch.[16]

It was entirely automatic. I did not hate the young man; I did not see him as the enemy; I did not ponder[17] issues of morality or politics or military duty. I crouched and kept my head low. I tried to swallow whatever was rising from my stomach, which tasted like lemonade, something fruity and sour. I was terrified. There were no thoughts about killing. The grenade was to make him go away—just evaporate[18]—and I leaned back and felt my mind go empty and then felt it fill up again. I had already thrown the grenade before telling myself to throw it. The brush was thick and I had to lob[19] it high, not aiming, and I remember the grenade seeming to freeze above me for an instant, as if a camera had clicked, and I remember ducking down[20] and holding my breath and seeing little wisps of fog rise from the earth. The grenade bounced once and rolled across the trail. I did not hear it, but there must've been a sound, because the young man dropped his weapon and began to run, just two or three quick steps, then he hesitated, swiveling[21] to his right, and he glanced down at the grenade and tried to cover his head but never did. It occurred to me then that he was about to die. I wanted to warn him. The grenade made a popping noise—not soft but not loud either—not what I'd expected—and there was a puff of dust and smoke—a small white puff—and the young man seemed to jerk upward as if pulled by invisible wires. He fell on his back. His rubber sandals had been blown off. There was no wind. He lay at the center of the trail, his right leg bent beneath him, his one eye shut, his other eye a huge star-shaped hole.

It was not a matter of live or die. There was no real peril.[22] Almost certainly the young man would have passed by. And it will always be that way.

---

11 **sandals** light, open shoes
12 **ammunition** bullets
13 **cocked to the side** bent toward his shoulder
14 **at ease** relaxed
15 **muzzle** shooting end of a gun
16 **I had come up to a crouch.** I had gotten on my feet low to the ground.

17 **ponder** think deeply about
18 **evaporate** disappear into the air (like water)
19 **lob** throw up into the air
20 **ducking down** dropping low to the ground
21 **swiveling** turning quickly
22 **peril** danger

Later, I remember, Kiowa tried to tell me that the man would've died anyway. He told me that it was a good kill, that I was a soldier and this was a war, that I should shape up[23] and stop staring and ask myself what the dead man would've done if things were reversed.

None of it mattered. The words seemed far too complicated. All I could do was gape[24] at the fact of the young man's body.

Even now I haven't finished sorting it out.[25] Sometimes I forgive myself, other times I don't. In the ordinary hours of life I try not to dwell on[26] it, but now and then,[27] when I'm reading a newspaper or just sitting alone in a room, I'll look up and see the young man coming out of the morning fog. I'll watch him walk toward me, his shoulders slightly stooped, his head cocked to the side, and he'll pass within a few yards of me and suddenly smile at some secret thought and then continue up the trail to where it bends back into the fog.

---

23 **I should shape up** I should get control of myself
24 **gape** stare amazed with an open mouth
25 **sorting it out** figuring it out
26 **dwell on** think a lot about
27 **now and then** occasionally

PART 1 FIRST READING

A Thinking About the Story

Discuss the following question with a partner.

In your view, who was the better soldier: the narrator or Kiowa? Explain your answer.

B Understanding the Plot

Be prepared to answer the following questions with a partner or your class.

1. What seems to be the narrator's current profession? How do we know?
2. What does the narrator's daughter ask him? How does he answer? How will his answer be different when she is older?
3. What detail indicates that the event described in the story takes place during the Vietnam War?
4. What do we know about the area where the soldiers are waiting? Give details.

5. What system do the soldiers use to watch for the enemy at night? (lines 18–20)
6. Roughly what time is it when the narrator first sees the young man?
7. Does the young man present a major threat to the narrator? Explain your answer as fully as possible.
8. What happens in the encounter with the young man?
9. Why does Kiowa tell the narrator to *shape up*? (line 70)
10. How does Kiowa try to convince the narrator to stop feeling guilty?
11. Does the narrator eventually learn to accept what happened? Explain your answer.

PART 2 CRITICAL THINKING

A Exploring Themes

Reread "Ambush." Then answer the following questions, which explore the story more deeply.

1. What are some of the long-term effects of war that the narrator examines in the story?
2. Why does the narrator feel the need to write war stories?
3. Read lines 44–48 and lines 57–58. Explain what they reveal about the narrator's thoughts and feelings when he is about to kill the young man.
4. What details suggest that the narrator was an inexperienced soldier?
5. What is the role of Kiowa in the story? How is he contrasted with the narrator?

B Analyzing Style

FRAME STORY

"Ambush" is a story within a story. This kind of narrative structure is like a painting, with a frame on the outside and a picture on the inside. Therefore, the story on the outside is often referred to as a **frame story**. The frame story gives a reason for telling the inner (main) story, which is where we focus our attention. Many classic stories are told in this way. For example, in the legend *One Thousand and One Nights*, a Persian queen must tell fascinating stories every night in order to stay alive.

In "Ambush," the frame story is about a man who is struggling with his memories of being a soldier in Vietnam. The inner story depicts a wartime incident from his youth that he has never been able to forget.

Exercise

Answer the following questions.

1. Summarize the frame story. (lines 1–10 and lines 75–83)
2. What is the mood of the adult narrator as he recalls the wartime event?
3. The inner story is related in one long paragraph. What is the effect of describing the incident in this way?
4. How would you describe the atmosphere in the inner story? What imagery helps create this atmosphere?
5. How do the setting and atmosphere of the inner story contrast with the setting and atmosphere of the frame story?
6. The narrator describes the young man twice in almost exactly the same words. The first time is in the inner story. The second time is in the frame story. How is the description different the second time? What is the significance of repeating the description with one change?

C Judging for Yourself

Express yourself as personally as you like in your answers to the following questions.

1. Do you think the narrator was right to lie to his daughter? Explain your answer.
2. Do you think the narrator's feelings about war reflect a typical soldier's views? Explain your answer.
3. Do you think that the narrator should feel guilty about what happened? Explain your answer.
4. "Ambush" reads like a real-life experience. However, we don't know whether this event actually happened to Tim O'Brien when he fought in the Vietnam War. Would it make a difference to you if you knew for sure that the story was or wasn't true? Explain your answer.

D Making Connections

Answer the following questions in a small group.

1. Have you or has anyone you know had military training or fought in a war? What effects did the military experience have?
2. How are soldiers treated in your country after they come home from a war? Do they get the help they need to return to civilian life?

3. Has your country been involved in a war during your or your parent's lifetime? If so, explain what it was about. If not, say why you think your country has avoided fighting.

4. Pacifism is the belief that no war is worth fighting. Are there people in your society who support this philosophy? Who are they? Why do they feel this way?

E Debate

Decide whether you are for or against the following statement. Write several arguments that support your view. Share your points with a classmate who has taken the opposite position.

There is no such thing as a just war.

PART 3

GRAMMAR IN CONTEXT

PAST TENSES

Since "Ambush" is about a character's memories, it is told primarily in the past. The narrator uses three **past tenses** to tell his story: the *simple past*, the *past progressive*, and the *past perfect*. He also uses the *present perfect*, which can act as a bridge between the past and the present.

1. The **simple past** describes an action, event, or state that started and finished in the past. For regular verbs, the simple past is formed by adding *–d* or *–ed*. However, many common verbs are irregular and do not follow this rule. The simple past of the verb *to be* is *was/were*.

   > The grenade **bounced** once and **rolled** across the trail. (lines 52–53)

   > . . . I **leaned** back and **felt** my mind go empty and then **felt** it fill up again. (lines 46–47)

   > It **was** not a matter of live or die. There **was** no real peril. (line 65)

   When a verb in the simple past is in the negative, it is formed by using *did* plus the base form of the verb.

   > I **did** not **hate** the young man. (line 40)

2. The *past progressive* describes an action or event that was in progress when another action in the past occurred. It is formed by using *was/were* plus the present participle.

   > We **were working** in two-man teams . . . and I remember it was still dark when Kiowa shook me awake for the final watch. (lines 18–20)

3. The **past perfect** describes an action, event, or state that had already been completed before another action in the past occurred. It is formed by using *had* plus the past participle.

> *When she was nine, my daughter Kathleen asked if I* **had** *ever* **killed** *anyone.* (lines 1–2)

> *I* **had** *already* **thrown** *the grenade before telling myself to throw it.* (lines 47–48)

> *I* **had** *only* **been** *in Vietnam for two weeks when I was wounded in battle.*

4. The **present perfect** is formed by using *has/have* plus the past participle. It describes an action, event, or state that has a connection with both the past and the present. The following are some of the ways in which the present perfect can be used:

- for an action, event, or state that began in the past and continues into the present

  > *Even now I* **haven't finished** *sorting it out.* (line 75)

- for an action, event, or state that happened at an unspecified time in the past

  > *I* **have been** *to both China and Vietnam.*

- for the number of times that an action or event has happened up to now

  > *I* **have read** *three books about the Cold War.*

- for an action or event that was recently completed

  > *I* **have** *just* **returned** *from Iraq, where I was reporting on the war.*

Exercise 1

In the following sentences, each verb in italics is in one of three tenses: the *simple past*, the *past progressive*, or the *past perfect*. Identify the tense. Explain why it was used in the sentence.

1. . . . she *knew* I'*d been* a soldier. (lines 2–3)
2. The night *was* foggy and hot. (line 21)
3. Very gradually, in tiny slivers, dawn *began* to break through the fog . . . (lines 25–26)
4. I *did* not *ponder* issues of morality or politics or military duty. (lines 41–42)
5. I *tried* to swallow whatever *was rising* from my stomach . . . (lines 42–43)
6. There *were* no thoughts about killing. (lines 44–45)
7. The grenade *made* a popping noise—not soft but not loud either—not what I'*d expected* . . . (lines 58–59)

Exercise 2

With a partner, explain the difference between the following sentence pairs.

1. **a.** We didn't see our brother last year.
   b. We have not seen our brother for a year.
2. **a.** The scientists at my university have just discovered a new star.
   b. The scientists at my university discovered a new star in January.
3. **a.** We have had many problems with our car.
   b. We had many problems with our car.
4. **a.** I was thinking about my wife when you came through the door.
   b. I thought about my wife when you came through the door.
5. **a.** We've watched two Steven Spielberg movies in my film class.
   b. We watched two Steven Spielberg movies in my film class.

Exercise 3

With a partner, complete the following dialogue with the correct tenses of the verbs in parentheses. Then say your dialogue out loud.

A: Do you like your history class this semester?

B: Yes. We _____ a lot so far about the Vietnam War. (read)

A: I took that class last year. One day, the professor

_____ about the war when a student

_____ arguing with him angrily! (lecture, begin)

B: I'm not surprised that people still feel strongly about the war. By the

time it _____ in 1975, more than fifty thousand

U.S. soldiers and hundreds of thousands of Vietnamese people

_____. (end, die)

A: It _____ certainly a very controversial period

in American history. (be)

B: At that time, almost everyone _____

a strong opinion about the morality of the war. Many Americans

_____ with the position of the government.

(have, not agree)

A: I _____ two classes about that period in history, but there's a lot that I still want to learn. Last semester the professor _____ out of time before he could talk about the long-term effects of the war. (take, run)

B: For me, the most interesting part of the class up to now _____ learning about the experiences of average soldiers. Most of them didn't choose to be in the war, and many were only teenagers when they _____ to Vietnam. (be, go)

Exercise 4

Complete the following sentences in your own words, using the tense indicated. The first is done for you as an example.

1. I _____was sleeping in my tent_____ when we received the order to attack. (past progressive)

2. The soldier with the radio said, "_____."
(present perfect)

3. I picked up my gun from the place where _____. (past perfect)

4. The captain yelled out his instructions, and _____. (simple past)

5. The enemy soldiers _____ when we discovered their position. (past progressive)

6. As my friend was getting out a grenade, _____. (simple past)

7. I was lucky that _____. (simple past in the negative)

8. My last break from duty was at Christmas. Since then I _____. (present perfect in the negative)

PART 4

VOCABULARY BUILDING

VOCABULARY IN CONTEXT

When you memorize a new word, it can be very helpful to connect it to its **context**. For example, the narrator in "Ambush" says: *In the ordinary hours of life I try not to dwell on it* . . . (lines 76–77). If you want to learn the verb *dwell on*, it may help to remember that the narrator dwells on his experience of killing the young man. In this context, it makes sense that *dwell on* means *think too much about*.

Exercise 1

With a partner, discuss the context in which the following words appear in the story. Then match each word to its definition in the right-hand column.

_____ 1. pretend (line 7)   **a.** danger

_____ 2. dense (line 16)   **b.** disappear into the air

_____ 3. ponder (line 41)   **c.** principles about right and wrong behavior

_____ 4. morality (line 41)   **d.** thick

_____ 5. terrified (line 44)   **e.** make a sudden movement

_____ 6. evaporate (line 46)   **f.** consider carefully

_____ 7. jerk (line 61)   **g.** act or think in a way that doesn't reflect reality

_____ 8. peril (line 65)   **h.** extremely afraid

Exercise 2

Complete the following sentences with the correct word from the left-hand column in Exercise 1.

1. The forest was so _____ that it was hard for the soldiers to see through the trees.

2. We were _____ when we found a poisonous snake in our tent.

3. Walking alone in enemy territory will put you in great _____.

4. When I was in the war, I would often close my eyes and _____ I was at home.

5. Recently, I've started to _____ what I should do after I leave the army.

6. I saw Kiowa _____ his head up when the missile passed above us.

7. During a battle, soldiers don't always have time to think about the
   _____ of their actions.

8. It rained heavily last night, but the water on the ground will
   _____ quickly in the hot sun.

FIXED EXPRESSIONS WITH *OR*

In a **fixed expression**, several words are used together as a single unit. English contains a number of fixed expressions that consist of two nouns, verbs, adjectives, or adverbs joined by the conjunction *or*.

In "Ambush" the narrator says that the encounter *was not a matter of **live or die*** (line 65). The sentence indicates that he did not absolutely need to kill the enemy. In this kind of expression, the word order is fixed. You cannot reverse the order and say *die or live*.

Exercise 3

Look at the following fixed expressions with *or*. With a partner, match each expression to its correct meaning.

_____ **1.** all or nothing   **a.** eventually

_____ **2.** heads or tails   **b.** mostly

_____ **3.** hit or miss   **c.** no middle position

_____ **4.** more or less   **d.** the only chance

_____ **5.** now or never   **e.** guess how the coin will land

_____ **6.** sooner or later   **f.** hard to predict

Exercise 4

Complete each of the following sentences with the correct expression from the left-hand column of Exercise 3.

1. To decide who would sleep first, Kiowa took out a quarter and said,
   "_____?"

2. Our guns were _____ useless in the dark.

3. All soldiers get sick in the jungle. _____, you will too.

4. Our information about the enemy is _____. You
   shouldn't rely on it.

5. One side in the conflict had an _____ attitude, so reaching an agreement was impossible.

6. Our opportunity to attack without being seen will only last for a few minutes. It's _____.

PART 5

WRITING ACTIVITIES

1. Some periods in history remain controversial long after they are over. Today, although most historians in the United States view the Vietnam War as a tragic mistake, some continue to argue that it was justified. Write a short essay about something in your country's history that divides public opinion. For example, it could be a law, a social movement, or a war. Say what happened and explain the different perspectives that people have today.

2. Choose something from your past that you've always felt guilty about. Describe the situation and explain why you acted the way you did. Pay attention to your verb tenses.

3. Films about the Vietnam War have explored the conflict from many perspectives. Some of the best-known ones include *Apocalypse Now, Full Metal Jacket, The Deer Hunter, Platoon, Born on the Fourth of July,* and *The Fog of War.* Choose a movie about the Vietnam War or another war. Describe the plot, and explain any issues that the movie helped you understand better.

Text Credits

Chapter 1
Katharine Weber. "Sleeping." Copyright © 2003 by Katharine Weber.

Chapter 2
Michael Plemmons. "Noel." Copyright © Michael Plemmons. All rights reserved. Reproduced by permission.

Chapter 3
Dorothy Parker. "Arrangement in Black and White." Copyright © 1927, renewed 1955 by Dorothy Parker. Originally appeared in the *New Yorker* magazine, from *The Portable Dorothy Parker* by Dorothy Parker, edited by Marion Meade. Used by permission of Viking Penguin, a division of Penguin Group (USA) LLC. Also reprinted with the permission of Gerald Duckworth & Co. Ltd.

Chapter 4
Raymond Carver. "A Serious Talk," from *What We Talk About When We Talk About Love* by Raymond Carver. Copyright © 1974, 1976, 1978, 1980, 1981 by Raymond Carver. Used by permission of Alfred A. Knopf, an imprint of the Knopf Doubleday Publishing Group, a division of Random House LLC. All rights reserved.

Chapter 5
Susan O'Neill. "Damn Irene." Copyright © Susan O'Neill. Previously published in *Indiana Review* (2005) and *You've Got Time for This*. All rights reserved. Reproduced by permission.

Chapter 6
Leslie Norris. "Blackberries," from *The Girl From Cardigan* by Leslie Norris. Copyright © 1988 by Leslie Norris. Used by permission of Brandt & Hochman Literary Agents, Inc. All rights reserved.

Chapter 7
Anthony Boucher. "Mr. Lupescu." Copyright © 1945 by Anthony Boucher. First appeared in *Weird Tales*, September 1945. Reprinted by permission of Curtis Brown, Ltd.

Chapter 8
Margarita Mondrus Engle. "Niña." Reprinted with permission from the publisher of *Short Fiction by Hispanic Writers of the United States* by Margarita M. Engle (Arte Público Press-University of Houston, 1993).

Chapter 9
Tayari Jones. "Some Thing Blue." Copyright © Tayari Jones. Reprinted with Permission.

Chapter 10
Patricia Grace. "Transition," from *Electric City and Other Stories*. Copyright © 1987 by Penguin New Zealand. All rights reserved. Reproduced by permission.

Chapter 11
Daniel Lyons. "The Birthday Cake," from *The Last Good Man* by Daniel Lyons. Copyright © Dan Lyons. Reprinted by permission of the author.

Chapter 12
Kate Chopin. "The Kiss" as found in *The Awakening and Selected Stories*. New York: Penguin Books, 1983.

Chapter 13
Armistead Maupin. "Letter to Mama." From pages 221–223 of *More Tales From the City* by Armistead Maupin. Copyright © 1979 by the Chronicle Publishing Company. Reprinted by permission of HarperCollins Publisher.

Chapter 14
William Saroyan. "The Last Word Was Love," from *Madness in the Family*. Copyright © 1988 by New Directions Publishing Corporation, © 1988 by The Saroyan Foundation, © 1988 by Leo Hamalian. Reprinted by permission of New Directions Publishing Corp.

Chapter 15
Jamaica Kincaid. "Girl," from *At the Bottom of the River* by Jamaica Kincaid. Copyright © 1983 by Jamaica Kincaid. Reprinted by permission of Farrar, Straus and Giroux, LLC.

Chapter 16
Tim O'Brien. "Ambush," from *The Things They Carried* by Tim O'Brien. Copyright © 1990 by Tim O'Brien. Reprinted by permission of Houghton Mifflin Harcourt Publishing Company. All rights reserved. Also reprinted by permission of HarperCollins Publishers Ltd.